Whatever Happened
to Local Government?

Whatever Happened to Local Government?

ALLAN COCHRANE

OPEN UNIVERSITY PRESS
Buckingham · Philadelphia

Open University Press
Celtic Court
22 Ballmoor
Buckingham
MK18 1XW

and

1900 Frost Road, Suite 101
Bristol, PA 19007, USA

First published 1993

A catalogue record of this book is available from the British
Library

ISBN 0 335 19011 1 (pb)

Library of Congress Cataloging-in-Publication Data
Cochrane, Allan.
    Whatever happened to local government / Allan Cochrane.
        p.   cm.
    Includes bibliographical references (p.   ) and index.
    ISBN 0–335–19011–1 (pbk.)
    1. Local government – Great Britain.   I. Title.
JS3118.C63   1993
352.041 – dc20   92–42634
                                                      CIP

Typeset by Type Study, Scarborough
Printed in Great Britain by St Edmundsbury Press Ltd,
Bury St Edmunds, Suffolk

To Margret

Contents

Acknowledgements

This book is informed by a long process of interaction with colleagues in the Social Sciences Faculty of the Open University, in particular with members of the Urban and Regional Research Group, but also others with whom I have worked on many course teams. They have taught me the need to look across a range of academic disciplines and to appreciate the value of critical comment within a process of collective endeavour. In particular, I would like to acknowledge the importance of discussion with others working on the South East Programme of research: they are John Allen, Julie Charlesworth, Gill Court, Chris Hamnett, Nick Henry, Linda McDowell, Doreen Massey, and Phil Sarre. John Clarke has been a continuing source of challenging ideas and supportive discussion. Both he and Christopher Pollitt have encouraged me to take the role of management more seriously. David Rosenberg opened my eyes to the importance of political processes within the state. I hope that my debts to others will be clear from the text which follows.

I am grateful to the Economic and Social Research Council for funding two pieces of research on the changing politics of local government. The results of the first – the effects of fiscal stress on budgetary processes in English local government (E00232131) – raised questions about the role of elite professionals within the local welfare state which have fed into the arguments developed below. Preparatory work and initial discussions on the second – local economic policy-making in a growth region (R000233007) – have encouraged a greater focus on forms of 'partnership' at local level. Although this book should not be seen as an attempt to write up the results of these projects, it could not have been written without them.

Some of the arguments developed in this book were first published in 1991 in *Public Administration*, 69(3), 281–302, in an article entitled 'The changing state of local government: restructuring for the 1990s'. Others were raised in a public lecture, 'Is there a future for local government?', given to the Centre of Regional and Economic Research at Sheffield City Polytechnic, which was subsequently published in 1992 in *Critical Social Policy*, 35, 4–19. The consideration of the experience of the community charge/poll tax first appeared as part of *From Poll Tax to Council Tax: the Short History of a Bad Idea* which was published in 1992 as a discussion paper from the Campaign for Rational Economic Debate by the Inland Revenue Staff Federation. I am grateful both for the permission to use material first published in these places and – possibly more important – for the opportunity of publishing in them in the first place.

Introduction

Not so long ago it was common for political commentators formally to acknowledge the existence of local government as vital evidence of the health of British democracy, before moving on (with a sigh of relief) to discuss more important matters, like the latest Cabinet reshuffle, the level of inflation, the state of the pound or the public sector borrowing requirement. Matters are no longer quite so straightforward. Since the mid-1970s conflict over local government spending and services has filled the front pages of national newspapers. Even the previously arcane issues of local government finance and local taxation have become important areas of debate. The failure of one attempt to resolve the problem of local government finance through the introduction of a new tax was the main factor which led to the resignation of a Prime Minister who had previously been viewed as almost all-powerful. At the start of the 1980s, few would have predicted such an outcome at the end of the decade. The 'low' politics of local government had come back to haunt the 'high' politics of Westminster with a vengeance.

There is a widely accepted fairy-tale about British local government in the last quarter of the twentieth century. It runs a little bit like this:

> Once upon a time there was something called local democracy. Every few years (every year in some places) people voted for their local councillors. These councillors ran the council with the help of appointed officials. Together they decided how to provide services to their local populations. In general the levels and forms of service provision reflected the demands of local electors. There was little conflict between central and local government, because each knew its place in the greater scheme of things. But then – around 1979 – the evil 'Snow Queen' came to power. She changed everything. Local electors were no longer able to make their own choices, because she – or her almost equally evil henchmen – made those decisions for them. She wanted to stop ordinary people receiving the benefits to which they had previously been entitled, and which had been promised to them by their friendly local councillors.

This fable seems to have two possible endings, depending on the storyteller. In one, the councillors and their professional allies succeed in turning the changes imposed from above to their own advantage – taking the opportunity to be self critical and to move away from well meaning but paternalistic bureaucracy towards a new world of openness and customer care. In the other, the witch triumphs – but is replaced by a lesser warlock – and local government is frozen in fear with all important decisions being made (heartlessly) in a high-rise palace in London.

Like all fairy-tales, of course, there are elements of truth in all this. No one could deny that the period since the mid-1970s has been one of major upheaval in local government, and it would also be difficult to deny that – in some sense at least – local government has been faced with a prolonged war of attrition from above over the past decade or so. Councils have faced severe financial pressures resulting from tight limits imposed from above, increased demands from below and the difficulties of raising sufficient local tax revenue (made more difficult by the introduction of the 'poll tax'). But it is equally important to acknowledge that the fairy-tale distorts as much as it clarifies. Most obviously, of course, it presents a remarkably rosy picture of the past, but most important, it tells us little about the major changes which have taken place, or why they have taken place. And, of course, it tends to cast local politicians (and sometimes professionals) in the role of innocent victims and even gallant heroes. Sometimes this may be justified, but too often it looks rather more like wishful thinking and special pleading. The changing face of local government through the 1980s (in its negative as well as positive aspects) owed as much to local politicians and officers as it did to the initiatives of central government, and – more important, perhaps – the changes can only be understood in the context of wider processes of economic and political restructuring, in which actors such as these have had limited room for manoeuvre.

There is widespread agreement that the position of local government within the British state system has changed significantly since the mid-1970s. Precisely what the nature of the change has been, however, and its likely future direction remain matters of serious contention. The aim of this book is to consider a wide range of interpretations of the changes which have taken place, and of the role of local government within that wider system. It sets out to develop a distinctive approach to those changes to explain what has happened and to point to likely future directions at the end of the twentieth century. It starts from the assumption that local government – or, more accurately, local politics – matters and that what happens at local level cannot (and should not) be left as a secondary and marginal aspect of the British political system. On the contrary, not only (paradoxically) are local politics becoming more and more important, despite the decline in direct service responsibilities held by local authorities, but also local forms of political accommodation between key social groups are pointing to new styles of political practice which are of much wider significance. A key question underlying the arguments of the book is whether forms of political accountability are changing to match these other shifts.

The book starts by considering the position of local government within Britain's post-war political system. The first chapter has four main aims: to explain the development of post-war local government in Britain as a part of the welfare state; to set out the main features which led to the period before 1979 being seen as one of relative growth and respectability (sometimes implicitly a 'golden age'); to question this interpretation, identifying tensions and weaknesses within it; and to outline some of the implications of seeing local government as part of the welfare state while still acknowledging the importance of its role within local politics.

The next two chapters turn to consideration of what can safely be described as the dominant interpretations of the changes of the 1980s and their implications for the 1990s. Chapter 2 considers debates which suggested that we were seeing the end of local government in the face of an inexorable process of centralization. Much of the academic writing on local government in the first half of the 1980s concentrated on arguing that central government seemed bent on its destruction and on the reimposition of hierarchical power relations. Academics were mobilized, or mobilized themselves, to defend 'local democracy'. This interpretation is questioned not only because the stated ambitions of the centralizers were not achieved, but also because the story of local government throughout the decade suggests that it retained an ability to develop new initiatives and resist pressures from above. The importance of policy networks within the state system in undermining hierarchical organization is emphasized.

The main thrust of the critique of local government which influenced the Thatcher Government was one which stressed the strength of market alternatives and the inherent weaknesses of bureaucratic organization. Chapter 3 summarizes these arguments (drawing on public choice theory) before going on to consider the extent to which they found effective expression in the 'reforms' of the 1980s, for example in the introduction of the community charge or poll tax, in moves towards the local management of schools, and the spread of the purchaser–provider model, particularly in community care. It is argued (following Le Grand) that, at best, there has been a move towards 'quasi-markets' which themselves are bureaucratically managed. This means that it remains necessary to develop a political analysis of the local welfare state. It is not possible to point to the operation of surrogate markets which are able to operate in the apparently neutral fashion of private markets in delivering public services.

If local government has not been replaced with central direction, nor by the market, yet substantial change has taken place, what are the main characteristics of that change? The three chapters which follow aim to answer that question. One feature of the rhetoric which accompanied the 'reforms' of the 1980s was the frequent use of the term 'enabling' (as used, for example, by Nicholas Ridley and Sir Roy Griffiths). This term has also been taken up and used not only by academics more sympathetic to local government, but also by strategic managers *within* local government, such as Rodney Brooke (now chief executive of the Association of Metropolitan Authorities). In Chapter 4 some of the positive, as well as the more negative implications of the term are considered, and it is argued that a strategic role for local government is by no means guaranteed, principally because of claims made by other agencies and because of the spread of inter-agency arrangements. It is difficult to see how councils can be in the position of 'enabling' others to act when they themselves are in a relatively weak position.

One of the weaknesses of the arguments discussed in the first four chapters is that they have tended to take local government for granted as a prime focus of attention. It is implicitly assumed that the task is to find a new place for it in a changing political context. But the context for change is wider than that and must include changes within the economy and society. Recent debates about moves from Fordism to post-Fordism have been particularly fruitful in producing arguments about the direction being taken by restructuring. Paul Hoggett and Gerry Stoker have written most interestingly in this area, and Robin Murray has tried to develop a strategy based on the possibilities apparently opened up by post-Fordism and 'flexible specialization'. Chapter 5 explores the debates and identifies the strengths of the arguments, but suggests that the use of these theories is ultimately unlikely to be very helpful since they encourage a distorted and undifferentiated view of the 'Fordist' past and imply a relatively straightforward transition from that to an unconvincingly flexible and differentiated future.

Building on the arguments of this chapter, Chapter 6 argues that it is necessary to explain the processes and directions of change in terms which focus on the restructuring of the British welfare state since the mid-1970s. The central argument is that the underlying assumptions of that state have been reshaped, so that welfare is increasingly defined in terms of the competitive position of places in the wider space-economy. Within this new framework, local (entrepreneurial) initiative is of greater importance and explicit welfare policies of less: to the extent that the latter increasingly need to be pursued in a 'business-like' fashion, with the political integration of the poor (and other users) through decentralized initiatives. The language (and practice) of partnership is increasingly important, including partnerships between the public and the private sectors, with non-statutory and voluntary agencies, with parents, with consumers and service users. The notions of local and urban corporatism (and growth coalitions) are used to explore these changes.

The concluding chapter reviews the arguments of the earlier chapters, stressing that the changes of the 1980s are not simply products of the Thatcher era. It sets out an alternative model for the 1990s, arguing that it is no longer possible (if it ever was) simply to focus on local government as an expression of local politics. On the contrary, the fragmentation of local government has led to a proliferation of different agencies which need to be considered as part of the local state, both in the fields of welfare and economic development. In a sense, therefore, the answer to the question posed in the title is that local government can now only be understood as one element alongside others within the welfare state. Analysis of local politics in Britain will increasingly need to be understood in terms which acknowledge this and consider the precise balance of political interests at local level, as well as the ways in which they are linked into wider policy networks and hierarchies of political, economic and social power. Elected local government will only be one element in locally-based political regimes, which will tend to be dominated by different forms of corporatist arrangement.

The book draws on a wide range of disciplinary approaches to develop its arguments – from debates within geography and sociology as well as political science and local government studies. It does so without apology, because it is only by bringing these approaches together that it is possible to begin to grasp the full significance of the changes which have been taking place and are likely to continue to take place through the rest of the century. The study of local government should not be left to single-discipline experts, because if it is its study will remain fragmented and (at best) we will only be able to understand parts of the story. The book also draws on a wide range of different theoretical approaches, particularly, although not only, from within Marxist and (neo)pluralist traditions, and (at the risk of accusations of eclecticism) sets out to justify and integrate them as the argument progresses. The Marxist tradition is particularly helpful in its identification of major processes of restructuring, rooted within a wider political economy, but is less helpful in following through the process of active politics at local level and within the state system. It is hoped that bringing them together in this way will make it easier to understand the changing shape of the local state as well as the possibilities and limitations of local politics in Britain in the last years of the twentieth century.

Chapter One

Local government as welfare state

In retrospect it is tempting to view the years between 1945 and 1975 as a 'golden age' for British local government, before the advent of Thatcherism and all its works. It was a time when spending appeared to rise almost inexorably and responsibilities were added incrementally in a way which seemed to make local government an increasingly important pillar of the British political system. It would be easy to conclude that the professionals and other workers employed by the councils were serving their communities efficiently and caringly with little outside interference, because such interference was unnecessary. A light haze of nostalgia should be enough to cover up any misgivings we might have.

But of course such a picture is misleading. 'Golden ages' are always extremely hard to find in practice, and local government has always played an ambiguous role, on the one hand helping to provide community support, while on the other being faced with the need to ration what is on offer. Even 'municipal labourism' as precursor (and later part) of the British welfare state found it hard to develop a heroic image, and was from the start associated with bureaucratic control as much as welfare provision. Popularism and 'little Moscows' were always exceptions rather than the rule (see Branson 1979 and Macintyre 1980). Bulpitt's comments on English local government between the wars is salutory in this context. He points out that 'Popular culture was either indifferent to, suspicious of, or directly antagonistic towards, elected local government' (Bulpitt 1989, p. 66). However romantically one views the past it would be difficult to claim that opinions changed significantly after 1945.

Although focusing specifically only on the experience of municipal labourism, Gyford neatly sums up the tensions at the heart of urban local government within the newly constructed welfare state:

> For all its faults municipal labourism, like the post-war welfare state of which it formed a part, secured considerable real improvements in the material conditions of working-class life. On occasion, however, it was prone to two weaknesses. It could display a certain heavy-handed paternalism, leading to an insensitivity to the self-expressed interests of ordinary people when these seemed to conflict with the plans or the enthusiasms of senior councillors or of professionals and other experts; and a certain introverted emphasis on political solidarity and discipline could sometimes blind local councillors to legitimate outside criticism, or could even be exploited for dubious ends . . . Usually it did the right things for people; but sometimes it could do the wrong things to people; and only rarely had it previously discussed either of those things with people.
>
> *(Gyford 1985, p. 10. See also the critically sympathetic*
> *discussion of Southwark in Goss 1988)*

Nevertheless the image of a golden age is not entirely misleading, particularly for those actively involved with local government. Until the mid-1970s, local government appeared to be a relatively unproblematic part of the British political system, despite attempts to 'modernize' it in the late 1960s and early 1970s. Its task was to deliver a fairly clearly defined set of services (including primary and secondary education, council housing and personal social services) at local level, reasonably efficiently and with a degree of (local) democratic accountability. It was not a subject of high political (or academic) controversy. Much discussion of local government started by emphasizing that it handled large budgets and was 'a multi-million-pound' business in order to show that it was an important part of the British state system, before going on to explain that despite low levels of voting in local elections it somehow had claims to being especially democratic (see the summary in Dearlove 1979, pp. 28–50).

The formal position of local government in Britain appears to place it at the bottom of a hierarchical structure of central–local relations (within a 'unitary state'). In principle (and law) the powers of local authorities are understood to be delegated from the centre, while 'the power to delegate or revoke delegated power remains in the hand of the central authority' (Rose 1982, p. 50). According to the old public administration orthodoxy 'Westminster and Whitehall provide the legal framework and exercise a general oversight but it is local people who make the rules work' (Hill 1970, p. 22). Within the nationally agreed framework locally elected councillors were expected to make decisions (in committees and council meetings) which were then implemented by professional officers (who also advised them). In practice, however, such a model fails to capture the reality of central–local relations and makes it difficult to understand the position of local government within the British political system. Despite the widely acknowledged importance of central power, it is misleading to believe that the centre can effectively control local government, at least as long as it exists as a separately elected and area-based system. Starting from the notion of a unitary state, and focusing on the legal framework, misses the importance of territorially-based political power (which is emphasized by Duncan and Goodwin 1988), as well as underestimating the extent of political independence available to non-central institutions in making decisions and allocating resources (see, for example, Gurr and King 1987).

It is also profoundly ahistorical, failing to acknowledge the incremental way in which local government developed, from below as much as by legislation from above. Although the county councils were created in 1888 they generally continued to be run by the same local dignitaries as in the past ran the Quarter Sessions, and many responsibilities now understood to be a part of local government (such as education and the administration of the poor law) were run by other agencies with little direct connection with central (or local) government. It was the growth of urban areas which helped to create councils looking more like those which were taken for granted until the middle of the 1980s. In the middle of the nineteenth century it was councils (such as Birmingham with the Birmingham Act of 1851) which used Parliament to extend their powers and incorporate more and more land. They began to undermine the cosy arrangements of the past and to put forward new models (see, for example, Fraser 1976 Conclusion, Lee 1963, pp. 21–43, Keith-Lucas and Richards 1978, pp. 12–13, Smith 1982, pp. 7–19). Indeed, Fraser argues that in the mid-nineteenth century, the 'natural location of politics' was the city, suggesting that it was only with the later involvement of the working class that political activity in Britain became dominated by a national agenda (Fraser 1976, p. 283). The models of the urban 'improvers' influenced the local government acts of the last decades of the nineteenth century. The new structures were not simply handed down from on high, which helps to explain why so many (61) county boroughs were left outside the jurisdiction of the county councils after the act of 1888. The British system may, therefore, be a hierarchical one but the way in which the hierarchy works in practice is the result of political processes of negotiation, rather than the product of legal or constitutional necessity.

More recently, the looseness of the principles underlying the division of labour between central and local government for the first 30 years after 1945 merely seemed to confirm the lack of controversy surrounding them. The convenient fiction was maintained that local councils were responsible for the allocation of resources at local level, as long as in practice they did not seek to challenge the position of central government and the priorities of central government departments. Bulpitt points out that, 'Like children [local authorities] were expected to be "good", respectable indoors and outdoors, and respectful to the centre. Misbehaviour was frowned upon, but its consequences were conveniently left unclear' (Bulpitt 1989, p. 66). In order to understand the changing position of local government – and the consequences of what came to be defined as 'misbehaviour' – it is first necessary to set the local government system in the wider context of the British welfare state.

THE RISE OF THE LOCAL WELFARE STATE

Two main periods of development can be identified up to the mid-1970s. The first, which stretches roughly until the early 1960s, saw local government consolidated as a key part of the British welfare state. The significance of this can sometimes be lost if too legalistic an approach is adopted. In the 1930s and 1940s elected local authorities lost many of the powers they had previously enjoyed. In 1934 they lost control over poor relief; in 1936 local responsibility for trunk roads was removed; in 1940 it was the administration of supplementary benefits which was removed; responsibility for hospitals was lost in 1946; powers to provide electricity supply were removed in 1947, and to provide gas in 1948 (this process is charted clearly in Dearlove and Saunders 1984, p. 381). Dearlove and

Saunders conclude that 'the clear trend was one of erosion of their responsibilities, and this has continued ever since' (Dearlove and Saunders 1984, p. 381). Dunleavy, too, stresses 'massive losses of local service control' as a result of the policies of the 1945–51 Labour Government (Dunleavy 1984, p. 54). As description these comments may be perfectly accurate, but the implication that local government was less important as an element in the state system of the immediate post-war period is highly inappropriate.

This is the case for two main reasons. First, it misreads the significance of the changes which took place, by implying that it was already existing local government services which were effectively 'nationalized', when in practice a new system was being constructed. The main arguments about welfare and industrial issues during and immediately after the Second World War were focused on rather different issues than local versus central control. On welfare the issue was whether and how to construct a system of universal benefits. Whatever the conflict between centre and some localities in the 1930s, no one would suggest that the social security system proposed by Beveridge was principally aimed at undermining troublesome local authorities, since, whatever its other faults, its stress was clearly on the provision of universal benefits coupled with a commitment to full employment (see Beveridge 1942). For the electricity and gas industries the issue was how to construct efficient industries capable of providing cheap fuel to industry (see Addison 1975, for a discussion of some of these debates). Certainly, there was a move away from localism in some policy areas as a result of this, but that was largely a consequence of seeking to introduce and develop a more universal approach, building on the experience of municipal collectivism, and operating on a much larger scale than had previously been possible, for example in the formation of the nationalized industries as public corporations along the lines of Morrison's London Transport. And the local provision of welfare was simply overtaken by attempts to generalize provision, instead of leaving it as a permissive patchwork. To focus on the ways in which local councils lost powers, therefore, is to miss the point. In almost all the cases listed by Dearlove and Saunders (certainly after 1945) the issue was not how to restrict spending in these fields, but rather how it might more effectively be extended and institutionalized.

It would also be a mistake to try to identify any clear logic underlying the decisions made about which responsibilities were to stay with local authorities and which were to be removed from them. In principle, it might have been reasonable to suppose that local authorities could have retained responsibility for the distribution of supplementary benefit or social assistance (as is the case in the Federal Republic of Germany), and that central government might have taken on responsibility for the primary and secondary education system (as is the case in France, whereas in the Federal Republic of Germany it is handled through the Länder). Until quite late in the day, it was still a matter of debate whether the National Health Service should be largely left to senior medical professionals to run, under the nominal control of appointed area boards, or be the responsibility of elected councils in joint boards (see, for example, Foot 1973, pp. 118–19, 131–3). But the process of reorganiz-ation at this time also suggested a substantial expansion of all the activities concerned – for example, taking over the voluntary sector as well as local authority run hospitals in the case of the NHS, the private as well as the local authority run electricity suppliers in the case of those industries, and launching a far larger system of social security, national insurance and unemployment benefit in the case of what had previously been poor relief. Those who continued to favour local or municipal control were generally also those opposed to the scale of reform involved. Although there remained a few determined localists (see, for example, Robson 1948, ch. 1), their views found little room for expression in the context of massive support for the new initiatives.

There is little contemporary evidence that the changes were introduced to undermine the power of elected local governments or to reduce local democracy. Concerns were expressed about some of the implications of council control of municipal enterprises (such as gas, water and electricity) but the fear was that this tended to encourage corrupt relationships between councillors, contractors and businesses and not that local democratic control was likely to result in any radical challenge to the centre. There is a danger of romanticizing arrangements which were effectively run at 'arms length', much like the multiplying autonomous agencies and direct service organizations of today, even if they were formally supervised by council committees (see, for example, Bulpitt 1983, p. 148). Bulpitt's interpretation of relations between central and local government in the 1920s and 1930s stresses the extent to which, particularly within the Conservative Party, but also more generally, local and national politics were divorced from each other, on the assumption that 'real' politics took place at national level, while local politics was a necessary evil through which welfare services were delivered with the help of central grants (Bulpitt 1983, pp. 147–55).

A possible exception to this broad conclusion is to be found in the restructuring of poor relief in the early 1930s, where the conflicts between local and central authorities are well recorded. There is substantial evidence from the inter-war period that local pressures were important in the generation of welfare provision at local level, with substantial variation between local authorities (see, for example, Branson 1979, Macintyre 1980, and Mark-Lawson et al. 1985). Even here, however, caution may be advisable since the extent of conflict is easy to exaggerate. From the perspective of the Labour Party, the 1930s can also be seen as a period of steady consolidation of municipal labourism (the confident rise of Morrison and the London County Council as the dominant model for Labour at local level), which implies a negotiated settlement between central and local government rather than a process of conflict and centralization (Gyford 1985, pp. 4–13). One plausible interpretation of the post-war reforms is that they built on and generalized some – although not all – of the initiatives pursued by the most active local authorities in the inter-war period, generalizing the Morrisonian dream.

The second reason why focusing on the removal of powers is misleading, is that it was accompanied by a massive expansion of responsibilities for local government within the welfare state which dwarfed previous levels of activity. In the 20 years after 1945, education and housing spending came overwhelmingly to dominate local authority budgets. By the 1950s, these together accounted for around 60 per cent of council spending, whereas in the 1940s, the figures were closer to 35 per cent (Dunleavy 1984, Table 3.2). And the sums of money involved had also risen dramatically in real terms. Overall spending by local authorities as a proportion of national income and the share of local spending as a proportion of government spending were also rising over the post-war period. Local authority spending as a proportion of national income rose from around 9 per cent in 1950 to over 13 per cent by the end of the 1960s, and as a proportion of public expenditure from around 26 per cent to nearly 31 per cent over the same period (Newton and Karran 1985, Table 1.7). Levels of local authority revenue spending almost quadrupled in real terms between 1940 and 1970 (Keith-Lucas and Richards 1978, Table 7.3). This suggests, intuitively at least, that the importance of local government was not declining over these years.

Equally important, perhaps, local government and its agencies became an increasingly accepted part of the everyday lives of most people after 1945. The 1944 Education Act ensured that most children attended local authority schools until the age of 15. Following the Town and Country Planning Act 1947, all new development proposals had to pass through a planning system based at local authority level. Meanwhile, increasingly large numbers of people lived in council housing, particularly in the wake of large-scale slum clearance programmes in Britain's major cities (there were 4.2 million council-owned dwellings by 1961, which accounted for 27 per cent of households. Hamnett 1992, p. 7). Although they were only brought together in specialist departments for the first time in the early 1970s, there was also a continuous growth of local authority-based personal social services, which were a practical expression of the 'cradle to the grave' supervision promised by the welfare state. The Children Act 1948, for example, significantly increased local authority responsibilities, beyond the poor law's provision for 'pauper children', moving away from the existing patchwork of voluntary charitable provision (Keith-Lucas and Richards 1978, p. 48).

Focusing on a supposed reduction in the powers of local government after 1945 makes it difficult to grasp the extent and direction of its post-war growth. Rhodes emphasizes that what he calls sub-central government (in practice mainly local government) 'was the prime vehicle for building the welfare state up to the 1970s' (Rhodes 1985, p. 40). And this is a point widely recognized, implicitly or explicitly, by others. Dunleavy effectively defines urban politics (he is reluctant to use the term local government) as the politics of what he calls 'collective consumption' (Dunleavy 1980). 'Collective consumption' covers those areas of state spending which are concerned with the reproduction of labour (but – at least for Dunleavy – not the direct transfer of income through social security or other benefit systems) rather than directly with production. Saunders' model of local government is also one which emphasizes its role on social consumption (or welfare) issues, even if his stress on the 'specificity' of local consumption politics makes it difficult to link them into the wider structures of the welfare state, which tend to be understood as being in the separate category of national politics (Saunders 1984). Like Dunleavy, Cockburn emphasizes the role of the local state in the process of 'collective reproduction' (Cockburn 1977). Such conclusions are vital in categorizing the first phase of post-war development, because they place local government at the heart of the post-war political compromise which has been called the Keynesian welfare state (see, for example, Mishra 1984, Offe 1984), and also provide a crucial context for understanding the restructuring of local government in Britain since the 1960s.

Councils increasingly had responsibility for the management of those aspects of the welfare state which required face to face 'professional style' involvement with people variously defined as clients, parents or tenants, even if the claims to professional status of many of the new professions remained uncertain. More straightforwardly rational-bureaucratic activities, such as the distribution of social security benefits, tended to be removed to national organizations while the health service (where the professional power of doctors was taken for granted) was also effectively removed from any vestige of democratic accountability. Local government was to be the home of the 'street level bureaucrats' (Lipsky 1979).

FROM MODERNIZATION TO CRISIS

Within local government, however, the professional prestige still remained with those departments which stressed the eternal verities of legal and financial rectitude, rather than those which were oriented towards the management of welfare state services. And the structure of local government remained the rather incoherent mishmash inherited from the nineteenth century, with rural districts, urban districts, municipal boroughs, county boroughs and county councils. These organizational forms fitted awkwardly into a welfare state with pretensions to universality. By the mid-1960s the uneasiness of this fit was increasingly apparent and attempts were made to correct it as part of the Wilson Government's broader programme of modernization.

A clutch of official reports and royal commissions at the end of the 1960s and the beginning of the 1970s concentrated on suggesting ways of improving managerial efficiency and 'streamlining' decision-making, within larger (more businesslike) authorities (the reports were generally known by the names of those who chaired the relevant committees: Maud 1967, Mallaby 1967, Redcliffe-Maude 1969, Wheatley 1969, Macrory 1970, Bains 1972, Paterson 1973). Each made similar points about the need for change, emphasizing the low calibre of officers and councillors and drawing on private sector management models to provide frameworks for change (see Dearlove 1979). The White Paper which set out the framework for reform argued that, 'Unless local government is organized to meet the needs of the future, and in particular is organized in units large enough to match the technical and administrative requirements of the services which it administers, its powers must diminish, and with it the power of local democracy' (HMSO 1970, para. 10). In England and Wales this debate led into the great rationalizing reform expressed in the 1972 Local Government Act, and legislation with similar ambitions was passed for Scotland in the following year. Bigger authorities were created, smaller councils merged to form new districts, regions and counties with unfamiliar names. In England, at least, the creation of metropolitan districts effectively created unitary authorities in urban areas, although this was obscured by the survival of metropolitan county councils, still looking for an increasingly elusive 'strategic' role for themselves until their abolition in the mid-1980s.

The dry legislative framework, however, only hints at the wider implications of change. The new structure was intended to go alongside and fit with a new managerial style. Setting up the new councils was expected to make it easier to break away from petty interdepartmental rivalries and to encourage the development of organizational forms more suited to strategic policy-making. Modernization meant that larger units were required and new forms of management (particularly corporate management) had to be introduced. This was the era of strategic planning, the creation of the metropolitan county councils and the Greater London Council (GLC) in England, and the formation of large generic social services departments. In the most 'progressive' authorities, there was a move away from departments to much larger directorates, and everywhere new chief officer management teams were set up and chief executives appointed (Dearlove 1979 Part 2 provides a valuable summary of debates current in the late 1960s and early 1970s; see also Benington 1976, Cochrane 1989, pp. 98–102, Cockburn 1977, chs 1 and 4). The Bains report on management structures combined detailed advice on appropriate management models with broad claims about an expanded role for local government. No longer were councils to be defined solely in terms of the services they delivered directly. Instead they were to be the managers of social and economic change in their communities. Local government, said the report, is 'not limited to the provision of services. It is concerned with the overall economic, cultural and physical well-being of the community' (Bains 1972, p. 122). Councils were to be the local strategic agencies of the welfare state (in the business of what Cockburn 1977 described as the management of people).

The attempted modernization of local government to fit its role as local expression of the welfare state is still clearer when the full range of reforms affecting it in the late 1960s and early 1970s is considered. In this period, extensive reforms were being introduced in secondary education which led to the development of comprehensive schools; this was the time at which the position of council housing (rather than private rented accommodation) as the main alternative to owner occupation was effectively endorsed (by 1971 31 per cent of households were living in council dwellings, replacing private rented accommodation as the second largest tenure grouping, Hamnett 1992, p. 7); reforms in town planning were introducing the interlocking system of structure plans and local plans which not only seemed to offer a more rational framework for development control, but also encouraged some planners to see themselves as having a leading (corporate) role in the development of council policies (see, for example, Reade 1987, pp. 59–62); most notably, perhaps, reforms in the personal social services were leading to the formation of social services departments and the creation of the generic social worker.

Social services departments are probably the clearest expression of local government as welfare state, with social workers as its professional representatives. The full recognition of social workers as 'professionals' is a relatively recent one, a product of the reorganization and expansion that took place in the 1960s and early 1970s. Even at the end of the 1950s most of those working in health and welfare departments of local government were untrained (although specialist qualifications were more common in children's departments) and it was not until 1962 that the Council for Training in Social Work (now the Central Council for Education and Training in Social Work or CCETSW) was set up to authorize courses in social work. In England and Wales the numbers graduating from recognized courses rose from 296 in 1960 to 2183 in 1972 and 3507 in 1980.

This belated professionalization is also a reflection of the length of time it took to move towards a more systematic organization of the local welfare state and of what came to be called the personal social services in particular. The unified social service departments set up within local government after 1970, effectively took over the social service responsibilities previously undertaken within children's, welfare, health and housing departments (as well as probation in Scotland). As in other areas of the local welfare state, the reforms followed from the reports of royal commissions – the Kilbrandon Committee Report on Children and Young Persons (Scotland) (published in 1964) and the Seebohm Committee Report on Local Authority and Allied Personal Social Services (published in 1968). The former led to the Social Work (Scotland) Act 1968, which integrated all forms of social work (including probation) in one local authority department and the latter to the Local Authority Social Services Act 1970, which had similar implications for England and Wales, although probation remained the responsibility of the Home Office. It was largely as a result of these reforms that there was such a large growth in the training and employment of social workers, and, effectively, the recognition of a new arm of the welfare state.

The period up to the early 1960s, then, was one of expansion and consolidation. The period between the early 1960s and the mid-1970s, was largely characterized by attempts to modernize local government, as part of a more extensive strategy of state-backed social and economic modernization, fostered first by the Wilson Governments of 1964–70, and then by the Heath Government of 1970–4. But the unwelcome reality for local government, and perhaps for social services departments in particular, was that just as the centrality of their role within the welfare state was accepted (just as, to paraphrase John Benington 1976, local government became big business), the whole pack of cards began to tumble down. It is one of the minor ironies of history that, just as social work managed to drag itself into the apparently calm waters of public sector professionalism at the start of the 1970s, all the certainties of the welfare state on which such professionalism was based themselves began to be undermined.

The crisis of local government was part of a wider crisis of the British welfare state. The nature of the crisis which affected the Keynesian welfare state, and its British version in particular, has been extensively discussed. Although there is some controversy about the roots of the problem, there is, at least, little disagreement that the old system was unable to sustain itself much longer. Indeed, there is substantial agreement between authors who agree on little else that the 1970s were a decade of crisis characterized by attempts to reduce levels of spending on welfare (see, for example, Johnson 1987, Leys 1989, and Mishra 1984). There is rather less agreement about how (and even whether) that crisis has been resolved. Looking a little more closely at the experience of local government – the local welfare state – may, therefore, also help us to approach some of the wider questions about the nature of the political restructuring which has been taking place. Paradoxically, this is made easier because the lateness of local government's full integration into the structures of the welfare state seems to mean that this time it has been at the forefront of change.

In retrospect, the period of attempted modernization looks like the last gasp of a social democratic political order whose leaders assumed that it would go on for ever. By the middle of the 1970s it was already clear that the favoured strategy could not succeed in a number of areas, particularly in the context of continued relative economic decline for Britain. The clearest expression of this was to be found in the need for the Labour Government in 1976 to draw on financial support from foreign banks and the International Monetary Fund, and – as a consequence – to accept the imposition of a strong deflationary package (as well as the first rumblings of monetarism). The commitment to the 'regeneration of British industry' through a strong industrial policy and the National Enterprise Board did not survive into the late 1970s (see, for example, Leys 1989, ch. 6 and Joint Trades Councils 1980). Mishra's comments about the crisis of the welfare state are also apposite for the particular case of local government: 'The state's ability to manage the mixed economy, of which the social welfare sector is an integral part, is in serious doubt. In many ways it is this loss of confidence which is at the heart of the crisis . . . The legitimacy of the welfare state is in serious doubt' (Mishra 1984, pp. xiii–xiv; see also Beer 1982).

RESTRUCTURING, LOCALITY AND POLICY NETWORKS

This conclusion provides the necessary starting point for an analysis of political change in the 1980s, but only the starting point. Jessop quotes Offe's comment that 'Capitalism cannot coexist with, neither can it exist without, the welfare state' (Offe 1984, p. 153, quoted in Jessop 1991, p. 105). This apparent paradox helps to explain some of the uncertainty and confusion which has surrounded the attempts to reform local government, because it helps to provide a context for those reforms. The 1980s represented an attempt to resolve the political (and economic) crisis bequeathed from the 1970s. For some the resolution was relatively straightforward, represented by the success of Thatcher as carrier of a new programme, whether understood as neo-liberalism, 'rolling back the state' or 'new times'. As the chapters which follow argue, however, it is difficult to accept that matters are or were as straightforward as such analyses suggested.

As Jessop argues, one consequence of having a welfare state was that some of those seeking paid employment no longer had to sell their labour at competitive market rates (so that labour-power instead of being bought and sold like a commodity was effectively 'decommodified'). The payment of benefits ensured that some people were able to stay out of the labourt market altogether, while the participation of others was subsidized in various ways. In the 1970s and 1980s the existing balance between welfare and capitalist labour markets became increasingly difficult to sustain. Jessop suggests that there are three principal (and different) strategies which may be adopted to resolve the problem – what he calls neo-liberalism, neo-corporatism and neo-statism. The first emphasizes 'the recommodification of labour-power, the privatization of state enterprise and welfare services and the deregulation of the private sector', so that subsidies and benefits will be reduced and there is little state intervention into the labour market. The second implies that 'economic and social affairs would be left neither to the market nor to the state: instead their governance would be delegated to various intermediary organizations'. The third 'would involve further decommodification to compensate for deficiencies in the market, an active structural policy to improve market forces and regulation to limit the operation of market forces', because the operation of the market itself is defined as the problem and a more consistent move towards decommodification is seen as part of the solution (Jessop 1991, pp. 95, 97 and 98). British local government in the 1980s was one of the major sites on which the battle between these options was fought.

The restructuring of local government in the 1980s can only plausibly be explained in terms which focus on the wider break up of the British welfare settlement, rather than terms which concern themselves largely with the detailed vagaries of change within elected local governments. Local government always fitted into the wider state system in more complex ways than suggested by legal formality or the orthodox analysis of traditional public administration. Such approaches helped both to obscure the role of interest groups at local level (even making pluralist analysis of local politics difficult) and the role of professional officers in policy formation at local level (and in negotiation with other levels of the welfare state).

Looking at local government as a local expression of the welfare state helps to undermine such approaches and to construct more convincing alternatives. Rhodes approach to central–local conflicts is a helpful starting point in identifying the importance of interaction within and between policy networks as part of the welfare state system. Although he acknowledges the relevance of territorial politics as one of the pressures which have helped to undermine the post-war arrangements, Rhodes is less concerned to identify anything specifically local about local government, or indeed to argue that any specific policy areas are appropriately (or necessarily) handled at that level. He refers to sub-national or sub-central government rather than local government as his object of study and stresses the contingent nature of political outcomes (see, for example, Rhodes 1985). His writing successfully highlights the significance of professionals within the political system, and is able to explain change and obstacles to it through the analysis of what is almost an enclosed political system, linking localities, and the departments of central government in a complicated web of negotiation and bargaining in which the various sides are not always clear, and there is often a high degree of confusion and uncertainty (see Rhodes 1988, particularly ch. 5, for the most developed expression of this approach).

The starting point of his argument is that the influence of the centre 'lies in its ability to cajole, bully and persuade (but not command), and even this ability may not call forth the desired degree of compliance'

(Rhodes 1988, p. 1). And his concern with sub-central governments (in which he includes the decentralized structures of central departments, the nationalized industries and ad hoc bodies or quangos as well as elected local governments) is not an apologetic one. On the contrary, he 'rejects a fixation on Westminster and Whitehall', believing that it does not help very much in answering the question: 'who gets what public services when and how?' (Rhodes 1988, p. 1). Answering that question adequately requires an analysis of sub-central governments as the deliverers of services as well as an exploration of the complexity of relationships between them and with the central institutions of the state.

Here, however, comes the first crucial point of his argument. There is, he says, no single centre. There are rather 'multiple centres or policy networks', each of which is centralized but between which there is little coordination (Rhodes 1988, p. 3). In other words, for Rhodes, it is, strictly, inappropriate to talk of 'central–local' relations as if there were a centre which could control local agencies. The system is more complex and fragmented than such a phrase suggests. For him, the system of 'central–local' relations is a product of many such networks, linking centre and locality often apparently independently of each other, but also influencing each other in ways which are rarely clearly understood by those involved.

Rhodes argues that there is a paradox at the heart of the British state system between the tradition which assumes that the centre knows best and the reality of the centre's dependence on local and other forms of sub-central government for the delivery of services. In other words, there is a fundamental tension within the system constructed so laboriously in the post-war period. And for him that tension can best be explored in terms of policy networks, which link the centre and localities, rather than by stressing the importance of local (or indeed, national) party politics. These policy networks can be defined as the systems of (vertical) linkages between professionals (and associated councillors) and civil servants responsible for policy within departments of central government. The point Rhodes makes most strongly is that the interests of these policy networks and the civil servants within them may not coincide with the interests of the government as a whole. Policy networks are service based and cut across hierarchies (being represented at different levels of government) within what Rhodes describes as a 'differentiated polity'. Each side of the network is dependent on the other: at local level officers are dependent for finance from the centre, and at national level civil servants (and ministers) are dependent on local officers for implementation. At central level departments (or parts of departments) may act as representatives of those they also manage. So, for example, the government may be arguing strongly for reductions in spending as part of an overall economic programme, while at the same time, civil servants within the Department of Education and Science, or the Department of Health, are arguing with their counterparts at local level for increased spending on particular schemes. The Department of the Environment is in a particularly uncertain position. In arguments with the Treasury, it is likely to support more spending in the areas for which it is responsible through local government, yet in its relations with local government it acts as the policer of budgets – indeed it effectively plays the Treasury role. And matters are made still more complex because, even in this context of departmental pressure for retrenchment, some parts of the department – those responsible for housing, planning and other spending areas – may also be encouraging increased spending. These internal conflicts of interest are reflected through policy networks.

There are separate networks in the fields of education, housing and social services which interact with each other in an uncoordinated fashion. The dominant level of government in the British system – particularly in England and Wales – is always likely to be the centre, since it is able substantially to influence the level of resources allocated and available to local government as a whole, and, now increasingly, to particular councils. But, as the Conservative governments of the 1980s discovered (see next chapter), it is not easy to control spending by edict.

Rhodes arguments are helpful in emphasizing the importance of policy networks – in highlighting the importance of politics within what is all too often seen as the 'black box' of the state machine – however much they may be constrained by the structural context (see also Jessop 1990, p. 345). But his reluctance to acknowledge the significance of the *local* aspects of local government except (through territorial politics) as an external threat to the running of the central–local system means that he underestimates a crucial aspect of the politics of local government within the welfare state. In this context, Duncan and Goodwin emphasize that the existence of local government 'with an electoral and democratic element' was a crucial part of the political settlement of the 1940s (Duncan and Goodwin 1982, p. 93). In other words, local government cannot simply be represented as the local welfare state, because it also has a genuinely governmental or political role, in the sense that it is used in some sense to represent and speak for interests defined as 'local'. It can make collective decisions 'which can be imposed even on those who do not agree with the decision' and has the 'task of balancing the different interests in society' (Stewart 1992, p. 33). In principle, of course, few would deny that there are differences between local authorities and local politics in different places. Such differences are frequently used to justify the existence of local government (John Stewart, for example, takes it for granted that local choice is important and sets out to find ways of making it achievable (Stewart 1983)). But in practice the implications of recognizing differences between places are frequently missed. Young and Davies, for example, point to the failure of the Widdicombe Committee (Widdicombe 1986) to pick up on the evidence of diversity between councils revealed by one of their own research studies (Leach et al. 1986, Young and Davies 1990, p. 60). Young and Davies go on to argue that 'the effects of locality seem all-important' although the main distinction they draw is between what they describe as rural and urban places (p. 61). What would it mean to take locality rather more seriously?

There has recently been an extensive debate arising out of the ESRC's Changing Urban and Regional System initiative about precisely how the notion of locality may (or may not) legitimately be used. At times this debate has generated more heat than light, but the books produced from within the projects have certainly provided some detailed evidence about the importance of exploring what is distinctive about political arrange-ments in different places. They have highlighted the importance of linking local social relations and local politics, as well as showing that local political institutions and actors within them have a significant degree of autonomy (see, for example, Cooke 1989a, Harloe et al. 1990). The results of the various projects associated with this initiative highlight important differences in the politics which dominate in the different localities. In Swindon, there has been a shift away from council-led economic development towards an acceptance that development consortia are likely to play a major part in the planning and development of new areas (Bassett and Harloe 1990); on Teesside the old corporatist arrangements have been found wanting with the decline of the chemical industry, but it is unclear what is likely to replace them – ICI continues to have a significant political role, an urban development corporation encourages a focus on property development and the local council is left to manage high levels of local unemployment (Hudson, R. 1990); in Cheltenham local authority strategies have reflected an alliance with the professional middle classes with development focused on anti-industrial prestige urban developments and the protection of the town's regency image (Cowen 1990); in Thanet there is a continuing conflict between different business interests mediated through the local council, which continues to promote tourism and port development, but also faces criticism over levels of spending from those outside the industry

(Pickvance 1990); on Merseyside (Kirby) the extent of business involvement is necessarily limited by the weakness of the local business sector and the lack of interest in development by the private sector, so that politics is more clearly oriented towards survival and community campaigning (Meegan 1990).

Duncan and Goodwin (1988, ch. 2) have more explicitly related notions of uneven development to debates about local government and the local state. Unlike others using the term, for them it is important that the local state is local. 'The uneven development of societies,' they argue, 'also means that class structures and other social relations are constituted spatially, sometimes in rather specific ways' (ibid., p. 73). And precisely because systems 'are spatially constituted and differentiated, it is necessary for state systems to respond with the development of local states' (ibid., p. 69). It is, they say, because local interests may take control of local states (reflecting local social relations) that conflict between national and local states is inevitable: in the first place, they argue that local states are necessary to reflect spatial divisions, but precisely because those divisions may begin to find expression in political terms then they also begin to challenge the more universal claims of the state at national level. The contradictory role of the local state as agent of and obstacle to the centre means that conflict is unavoidable (ibid., chs 5 and 8)[1].

Warde's more modest formulation is helpful in emphasizing the significance of local context 'as a constraining or empowering condition of action' (Warde 1989, p. 279). He emphasizes the way in which 'a configuration of institutions and forces comes to exist at a determinate point in space and time, and that provides the conditions in which people are obliged to make their own history' (Warde 1989, p. 280). Elsewhere Warde's use of the term 'local political environment' highlights some of the ways in which context may be important in the analysis of local politics, because 'It implies a notion of incremental change, of one element affecting another . . . the environment structures the agenda for all political actors, setting the agenda for interaction between all parties' (Mark-Lawson and Warde 1987, p. 229). Massey's approach to the analysis of economic development is helpful here, since it stresses the ways in which layers of development build up, each previous layer influencing the next, in such a way that each place becomes unique, yet is also influenced by wider processes of economic development (Massey 1984, pp. 117–18). The notion of layers of development is not one which has to be limited to discussions of the economy. On the contrary, although a focus on the economy is a useful starting point, because it makes it possible to show the model in a relatively simplified form, any developed analysis of the way in which places develop a distinctive identity needs to consider the ways in which the economy relates to other aspects of our social existence. How a local economy develops will itself be influenced by local social relations and local political relations (as well as by their interaction with national and international levels). And, of course, local social structures and political practices will also be influenced by the nature of the local economy and its history. Localities are the products of interaction between people, groups and institutions in particular places over time. And this interaction is influenced by legacies (even memories and representations) from the past.

If Duncan and Goodwin overemphasize the necessity of analysing local government as an expression of uneven development within capitalism, Rhodes seems to underestimate the significance of these factors. As we have argued above, he finds it difficult to give independent weight to political developments at local level. Rhodes generally tends to play down the significance of the ways in which the operations of policy networks he describes fit into wider processes of capitalist development. They appear to exist in a separate system of their own, even if it is sometimes buffeted by external pressures. Yet in the end the system clearly breaks down under the impact of just these wider economic and political pressures, which encouraged the 'squalid' intervention from the centre which he describes (Rhodes 1985). Duncan and Goodwin may exaggerate the extent to which the operation of local government can be explained in terms of processes of capitalist development, but Rhodes underrates their significance. Separately the approaches of both Duncan and Goodwin and of Rhodes have significant weaknesses. But their arguments may be complementary rather than necessarily contradictory and in what follows we hope to draw on both of them to provide an alternative way forward through the analysis of local politics in the 1980s and into the 1990s.

The notion of 'urban regimes' (Stone 1987) offers a way of bringing the two sides of the local welfare state together, although its US origin means that there may be a danger of underestimating the significance of intra-state policy networks of the sort identified by Rhodes. Stone defines 'urban regimes' as 'the informal arrangements by which public bodies and private interests function together in order to be able to make and carry out governing decisions' (Stone 1989, p. 6). Keating builds on this to suggest that urban regimes consist 'of constellations of public and private power within a structurally defined context. Public policy is seen as the outcome of both economic and political power, with the composition of each and the balance between them varying among cities' (Keating 1991, pp. 7–8). In the British context, it seems legitimate to relate this formulation to localities as well as to 'cities', particularly since it fits well with some of the findings reported from the ESRC projects referred to above. Most of Britain's localities (even the most apparently 'rural') are, by now, effectively parts of wider urban systems (Dunleavy 1981, pp. 2–6). It also fits well with Jessop's argument that the (capitalist) state is best seen as:

> a strategically selective terrain which can never be neutral among all social forces and political projects; but any bias is always tendential and can be undermined or reinforced by appropriate strategies. For, within the strategically selective limits established by state structures and operating procedures, the outcome of state power also depends on the changing balance of forces engaged in political action both within and beyond the state.
>
> *(Jessop 1990, p. 253)*

Although there is no absolute logic of capital to be unambiguously translated into state form, or political initiative, the structural constraints implied for politics by the capitalist state form are real enough: above all in the way in which the division between private economy and the state means that the latter remains dependent on the private sector as the source of economic well-being (Jessop 1990, pp. 178–80). The arguments which follow will therefore set out both to explore the changing nature of the 'constellations of public and private power' within British local government in recent years and to place them clearly within their changing 'structural context', both as part of the local welfare state and within a wider process of economic and social restructuring.

NOTE

1 More recently Duncan has argued strongly that the notion of 'locality' is fundamentally flawed since it implies that places may be 'autonomous subnational social units' (Duncan 1989b, p. 247). On the contrary, he argues that localities in this sense are rare and that use of the term tends to be misleading, encouraging what he calls spatial determinism – that is the view that 'spatial patterns cause social behaviour' (ibid., p. 221). Despite his distrust of 'locality', however, Duncan continues to stress the importance of spatial variation, noting both the importance of what he calls spatial contingency effects and local causal processes. All social processes are influenced by spatial contingency effects because they develop (are constituted) in particular places and are therefore influenced by their interaction with pre-existing spatially

variant economic, social and political forms. In some cases, he says, it is also possible to identify causal processes generated at local level, because 'determining social systems are spatially variant, and because actors monitor and respond to their variable contexts' (ibid., p. 247).

Chapter Two

The 'end' of local government?

Until the middle of the 1970s local government in Britain was a political backwater. Local politics seemed to arouse little electoral interest. There was little open conflict between central and local government and the great debates about local government reorganization failed to strike much of a chord outside the narrow confines of the academic and local government policy communities, except when they threatened the continued existence of traditional county names (such as Rutland or Yorkshire). After the mid-1970s, however, things changed dramatically. Local government became the target for a whole series of 'attacks' (or reforms) from above. Whether they wanted to or not, local politicians and officers were drawn into high profile controversy over spending levels, tax levels, service reductions and efficiency savings. The various grant regimes and methods of calculating Grant Related Expenditure Assessments (GREAs) and Standard Spending Assessments (SSAs), coupled with powers to cap first rates and later community charge (and council tax) levels, suggested a significant increase in central political power, and the bureaucratic power of the Department of the Environment and its officers, at least as far as individual local governments were concerned. Levels of conflict between central and local government increased and at local level there was a rise of new politicians and an increase in locally-based campaigning over a wide range of issues (sometimes described as 'new social movements').

MOVING TOWARDS CENTRALIZATION

The 'attack' on local government predated the election of the first Thatcher Government. It was an expression of the crisis of the Keynesian welfare state and the particular problems faced by Britain within the global economic system (see, for example, Harris 1988, Brett 1986, ch. 6). Local government was among the earliest areas to be hit by the new financial restrictions, which were as much concerned with reducing overall tax burdens (including local taxes) as with the Public Sector Borrowing Requirement about which there was so much obsessive discussion at the time. As early as 1975, Tony Crosland, then Secretary of State for the Environment, announced that cuts were needed in local government spending: 'We have to come to terms with the harsh reality of the situation which we inherited. The party's over' (quoted in Crosland 1983, p. 295). The first signs of change were to be found in the reduced level of grants paid by central government to cover the costs of local authority expenditure. This reached a peak in the mid-1970s – with 66.5 per cent of revenue-based local government expenditure being payable as grant in England and Wales and 75 per cent in Scotland in 1975–6. By the start of the 1980s proportions had fallen to 61 per cent and 68.5 per cent respectively (Cochrane 1989, Table 4.2)[1]. It was the start of a period (stretching into the mid-1980s) characterized largely by attempts to increase central control over local government finance.

Although – as we shall see below – there is substantial doubt about the extent to which this centralization has been successful, there can be no doubt that the end result was an increased involvement of the departments of central government (in England, particularly the Department of the Environment) in the details of local government finance. Rhodes points to the way in which the 'pre-eminence of the Treasury and the treatment of *local* expenditure as a matter for national decision' became taken for granted within government (Rhodes 1986, p. 239). And by the mid-1980s in England and Wales the Department of the Environment had taken on the rather uneasy role of being advocate of spending on local authority services within central government, while setting out to control actual levels of spending at local level (acting – at least as far as local governments were concerned – as a surrogate for the Treasury) (ibid., p. 238). In Scotland the Scottish Office took on similar roles, possibly with a greater enthusiasm for that of the Treasury to the extent that Goldsmith argues that it acted as 'pioneer for the Imperial core, seeking and using greater controls over local government' than was the case in England (Goldsmith 1986, p. 168).

Although the process of increasing control and the imposition of stricter financial limits started in the 1970s the methods changed significantly between the 1970s and 1980s. During the 1970s controls were generally imposed through limits to overall levels of central government grant and the use of 'cash limits' (making little allowance for inflation). The local authority associations discussed overall levels and directions of spending with central government through a Consultative Council on Local Government Finance. According to Rhodes this council 'was successful in getting the local authority associations to persuade their members to behave with restraint' (Rhodes 1992, p. 53; see also Rhodes 1986). At first this seems to have been relatively successful – at least from the point of view of central government – since local government spending as a proportion of domestic expenditure fell sharply from 12.2 to 9.6 per cent between 1975 and 1979 but then stabilized until the mid-1980s (Department of the Environment 1992, Table 34). Because councils still had the option of raising money locally through the rates this is in practice what they did to maintain levels of spending (and services). Overall levels of spending did not fall as much as might have been expected, but the proportion funded by grant – as we have seen – fell dramatically. In other words a higher proportion of local authority spending was funded through local taxation.

Signs of more direct controls were already apparent in some key areas, however, particularly over capital expenditure (and the raising of funds for capital spending). In the case of housing, patterns of capital spending in England and Wales had to be agreed with the Department of the Environment through Housing Investment Plans, and similar arrangements existed for transport spending (including roadbuilding). In arrangements which prefigured those which were more commonplace at the end of the 1980s, following the Inner Urban Areas Act of 1978 urban programme spending was organized through locally-based partnerships (involving the private as well as the public sector) which also involved the departments of central government more directly in decisions on longer-term patterns of spending (Lawless 1989, ch. 3).

If the direction of change was already clear at the end of the 1970s, the *pace* of change accelerated dramatically with the election of the first Thatcher Government. An apparently never-ending series of changes (which caused local authority treasurers to complain about uncertainty as much as fiscal stress) brought further controls on capital and current expenditure. The changes were heralded by the Local Government Planning and Land Act (1980), which introduced a new block grant in England and Wales and included a formula which penalized councils which spent more than a previously determined limit. Grant was removed from those authorities, so that any increase in spending brought a fall in income and, therefore, implied a further increase in rates to make up for that loss. Now councils were to be targeted individually rather than as a group. This was taken further with legislation which limited rate levels as well as spending. The first steps in this direction were taken in Scotland in 1982–3 when individual councils were targeted for 'excessive and unreasonable expenditure' in what was popularly labelled a 'hit-list' (see Midwinter, Keating and Taylor 1983). Legislation on 'rate-capping' was enacted in England and Wales in 1984, making it possible for the first time for central government to set a maximum level of local taxation for particular councils. The naming of the councils to be capped (or at risk of capping) became an annual ritual, even if it was not always clear quite how the various calculations of GREAs and, more recently, SSAs on the basis of which councils were to be targeted had been made. As if to confirm that it meant business the government also abolished the Greater London Council (set up in 1963) and the Metropolitan County Councils (created in 1974) in 1986.

The overwhelming academic consensus about local government in the early 1980s seemed relatively straightforward. It was that the various 'reforms' being introduced by the Thatcher Government were fundamentally undermining the position of local government within the British political system. It was identified as a period of centralization, and one in which the changing rules of finance were fundamentally, probably fatally, undermining the scope for local autonomy. This view was endorsed by a range of authors from a wide variety of theoretical positions. The most enthusiastic defenders of local democracy were probably those closest to the local government community, such as SAUS 1983 and Jones and Stewart 1983, who saw themselves as making the case for local government. It was argued that 'decentralized democratic decision-making in the form of representative local government is an essential element of the county's political and government system . . . we believe the government's proposals to limit local authority rates and expenditure levels are a major threat to this' (SAUS 1983, Conclusion).

According to Stewart, 'in place of local choice will be the decision of the Secretary of State who is seeking . . . remarkably unrestrained power' (Stewart 1984, p. 9). It was claimed by some that the, in retrospect rather limited, provisions of the Local Government Planning and Land Act marked 'the beginnings of the wholly centralized state' (Burgess and Travers 1980, p. 188). Others commented that, 'the British system of government was already highly centralized in 1979, and subsequent legislation has produced a quantum jump towards a more powerful and centralized state,' and went on to suggest that, 'Britain stands in sight of a form of government which is more highly centralized than anything this side of East Germany' (Newton and Karran 1985, pp. 121 and 129).

Similar arguments came from authors taking rather different theoretical positions, who tended to speak of the local state rather than local government. Saunders identified a series of mechanisms through which central government tried to limit local government initiative and control its spending, to shift the balance of power in favour of the centre, also noting, however, that these attempts to increase control were only partially successful (Saunders 1984, pp. 32–8). He stressed the greater openness of the local state to pluralist pressures as a potential threat to the more corporatist arrangements which existed at the centre. Local government was also defended by Duncan and Goodwin who argued that it was under attack because it was an institutional expression of uneven development – itself a necessary consequence of capitalist development. Within their model, the existence of the local state implied the possibility of alternative political bases to the central organization of the capitalist state, and to Thatcherism in particular, and meant that conflict was inevitable, 'so that alternative interpretation and effective representation of oppositional voices is stilled' (Duncan and Goodwin 1988, p. 275). The analysis developed by Duncan and Goodwin suggested that the conflict between central and local government was likely to be resolved at the expense of local government (Duncan and Goodwin 1988). Gurr and King also pointed to increasing centralization in the 1980s, stressing what they saw as a range of tendencies increasing the power of what they described as the central state (Gurr and King 1987, pp. 180–4).

Whatever the label, then, whether councils were identified as part of the local state or local government, the academic consensus was not only that they were losing their scope for autonomous action in the early 1980s, but also that they were losing it in favour of a much more centralized system. The apparently obsessive search for 'overspenders' had necessarily involved a greater and greater emphasis on finding ways of imposing centrally determined rules about what was permissible and of devising methods of gathering evidence about the spending of individual authorities.

THE FAILURE OF CENTRALIZATION

Despite the attempts to increase central control, however, it is the difficulty central government had in achieving these ends, even in the high period of centralization as a strategy, which is most striking. By the middle of the decade it was apparent that many of the more direct assaults on local government had not been very successful in their own terms – it was, for example, increasingly clear that neither levels of spending nor employment (particularly white-collar employment) had decreased significantly. In England, despite a decline in capital expenditure (spending on equipment, buildings and infrastructure financed by long-term loans) by 50 per cent[2], current expenditure (spending on services, mainly financed by tax and grant income and short-term loans) actually rose (by around 13 per cent) in real terms from 1981/2 up to 1989/90. Even when account is taken of the fact that inflation is higher for local government than in the economy as a whole (as reflected by the retail price index) it is apparent that spending also rose in volume terms (by 7 per cent between the same years) (Department of the Environment 1992, pp. 10–11). In Scotland it has been calculated that between 1979 and 1988 the volume change in spending was 3.2 per cent (Midwinter 1988, p. 22). Local government expenditure as a proportion of total UK state spending and as a proportion of domestic expenditure also remained much the same over the decade. In 1990/91 it still accounted for nearly 30 per cent of all public expenditure, if anything having risen slightly over the decade (Department of the Environment 1992, p. 50), and although it had fallen slightly as a proportion of domestic expenditure (from a peak of 9.7 per cent in 1981 to 8.7 per cent in 1990) this can partly be explained by the vagaries of economic growth and the business cycle (since it represented a smaller share of a bigger total at the end) (Department of the Environment 1992, Table 34). (See Figure 1.)

The numbers employed in local government also rose, although there was a decline in the employment of manual workers and a growth in part-time working (Fleming 1989). Local government employment as a proportion of the employed labour force actually rose between 1970 and the end of the 1980s (from 10.3 per cent in 1970 to 12.0 per cent in 1988) (Pickvance 1991, Table 3.3). In England the numbers employed when translated to full-time equivalents fell by around 89,000 (4.5 per cent)

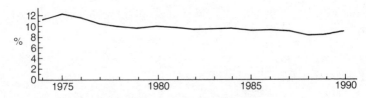

Figure 1 Local authority share of all domestic expenditure (UK) (*Source:* Department of the Environment (1992), Figure 9, p. 12).

between 1979 and 1991, but the significance even of this minor drop should not be exaggerated, since it includes staff in the polytechnics, staff previously employed by the Greater London Council and the metropolitan county councils and municipal employees associated with the bus industry and airports. These account for some 60,000 of the jobs lost. Meanwhile, the numbers employed in the personal social services, housing, and law and order increased throughout the decade (Department of the Environment 1992, p. 13). (See Figure 2.)

The purpose of emphasizing the limits to financial centralization is not to minimize the changes which took place, nor to underestimate the difficulties faced by local authorities throughout this period. This was not a time of budgetary expansion, yet it was a time in which demands on the local welfare state increased, not least because of the growing numbers of old people, the impact of significant levels of unemployment and growth of poverty through the decade (see, for example, Cochrane 1993). In some areas the changes had a more dramatic impact than in others. Capital expenditure on housing by local authorities was reduced to a trickle, encouraging a shift to owner occupation (if not the hoped for revival of the private rented sector) and incidentally encouraging an increase in levels of homelessness (Skellington 1993). In real terms, capital spending by local authorities on new house construction fell by 83 per cent between 1976/7 and 1987/8 (Hills and Mullings 1990, p. 158). In personal social services on the other hand, local authority current spending rose through the decade virtually matching the fall in capital spending, which suggests a changing strategy towards the area, rather than a desire to reduce spending (Evandrou et al. 1990, p. 219). In terms of employment – as we have seen – the numbers of manual workers fell sharply, particularly with the rise of contracting out but also with the decline in construction work. More white-collar workers were employed, almost ensuring that overall levels of employment remained the same (Fleming 1989). Such changes clearly are important, even if they do not seem to fit into analyses suggesting the 'end' of local government.

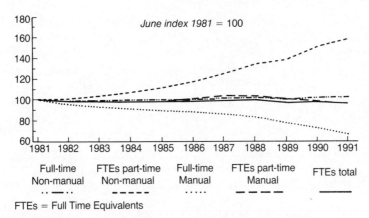

Full-time Non-manual ·· — ··
FTEs part-time Non-manual — — — —
Full-time Manual · · · · ·
FTEs part-time Manual — — — —
FTEs total ——————

FTEs = Full Time Equivalents

Figure 2 Trends in local authority staffing (England and Wales) (*Source:* Department of the Environment (1992), Figure 10, p. 13).

The trend towards a reduction in the proportion of expenditure funded by central government grant continued until the end of the 1980s and by 1989 only 43.9 per cent of local authority expenditure (in this case including capital expenditure) was covered by grant compared to 47.5 per cent in 1981. Income from the rates was covering 36.3 per cent (with an additional 1.1 per cent in domestic taxation already being met by the community charge) compared to 31.8 per cent in 1981 (Central Statistical Office 1992, Table 6.19). If current expenditure alone is taken into account, then the share funded by grant falls from 49.3 per cent in 1981 (51.9 per cent in 1979) to 46.4 per cent in 1989, and the proportion paid for out of rates (and community charge) rises from 33 per cent in 1981 (29.5 per cent in 1979) to 38.4 per cent in 1989 (Central Statistical Office 1991, Table 8.1). Pickvance suggests that, since the administration and payment of housing benefit became a local government responsibility in November 1982 but is funded directly by central government (through first the Department of Health and Social Security and now the Department of Social Security), strict comparability between the start and the end of the decade should discount that element of the grant, so that the shift can be seen to have been greater still (Pickvance 1991, p. 57).

Even without such an adjustment, however, it should be clear that there was a continuing move towards paying for local government from local taxation, which in 1989 still included domestic and non-domestic (i.e. business) rates. In other words, local authorities chose or – some would argue – were effectively forced to raise local taxes to maintain services and spending levels. In England local authorities consistently spent above the level of provision in the government's rate support grant settlement, at levels ranging from £0.6 billion in 1983/4 to £2 billion in 1986/7. In 1989/90, they spent £1.4 billion more (around 5 per cent more than the government's provision) (Department of the Environment 1992, p. 12). Midwinter provides similar evidence from Scotland, where the 'overspend' ranged from 4.7 to 3.2 per cent of government provision between 1983/4 and 1987/8 (Midwinter 1988, p. 22).

LOCAL RESISTANCE AND LOCAL VARIATION

Some of the mechanisms of central control actually had the opposite effects to those which were intended, to the extent that not only was spending encouraged to rise, but also the information passed back to central government became more and more unhelpful with the growth of 'creative accounting'. Attempts to impose increased central control in effect encouraged an organizational culture at local level which reinforced attempts at evasion (see, for example, Stoker 1991a, ch. 7). One of the Audit Commission's early reports argued strongly that previous attempts to calculate GREAs on the basis of which grant was allocated to and withheld from local authorities actually forced up spending and increased rate levels since they encouraged councils to build up reserves and balances to deal with future uncertainties. The report questioned the ability of central government to make accurate estimates of necessary expenditure at local level and suggested that figures on expenditure which were supplied by local authorities (and on the basis of which central estimates are made) were becoming seriously misleading because they were being 'massaged' to fit in with what the Department of the Environment wanted to hear (Audit Commission 1984). It was possible to manipulate accounts so that 'spending' could take place in one year rather than another, and to change definitions of what was capital and what current expenditure. Special accounts could be identified for specific purposes and carried over from year to year (money in such accounts could always be vired back into the main rate fund account at a later date).

In some respects the story of the 1980s is a story of attempts by the centre to plug loopholes in financial conventions while local authority treasurers searched for ways of finding new ones (see, for example, Clarke and Cochrane 1989, Stoker 1991a, pp. 174–6). The story of 'lease/lease back' schemes is instructive here. These effectively made it possible to borrow from the private sector without having to get permission or apparently to borrow money at all (at least as far as the accounts were concerned). Council property was sold on a long lease to another agency and then leased back until the long lease expired. It was, therefore, possible to get an immediate cash injection while retaining the property in practice (although, of course, it implied a continuing financial commitment in the form of rent). Such schemes were particularly attractive to councils with significant capital assets but heavily squeezed in terms of current income. The rules surrounding these deals became more and more complicated through the decade, until they were finally outlawed in 1987. By the end of the 1980s 'creative accounting' no longer had quite so high a profile as a way out of immediate difficulties, both because many councils were having to pay for the costs of past deals and because some schemes (such as swap transactions which involved councils speculating on the future directions of interest rate movements) had been declared unlawful. But the principle of maximizing grant and other sources of income by seeking to evade the controls of the centre and looking for accounting loopholes was simply taken for granted, even in the most respectable of Conservative controlled authorities.

The apparent failure of the centralization strategy also reinforces the importance of focusing on local government as part of a more complex state system – and in particular as a local expression of the welfare state. It tends to support Rhodes' argument that there are overlapping networks of bargaining linking different levels of government, with each level dependent on the other to achieve its own ends, in ways which sometimes encourage inconsistency between different parts at each level. It reinforces the conclusion that there is an inherent conflict between the assumption within the British state system that the centre makes the final or authoritative decisions and a practice which implies a high degree of interdependence and a complex process of interaction, organized through policy networks (Rhodes 1981, 1988; see also Laffin 1986).

The value of Rhodes' model can be seen clearly in the lessons he draws from the experience of the 1980s, when conflicts between central and local government were at their most marked. He argues that:

1 Changes in the central–local government system were not the product of any one process (such as economic decline) but of interaction between a number of processes. One which he identifies as important was the tension between Britain's economic decline and the institutionalization of interests within policy networks, which made it difficult to translate economic priorities into changes within the spending arms of the welfare state;

2   The conflicts of the 1980s were not simply the product of Conservative government policies, but of the longer-term piecemeal accretion of responsibilities at local level, which encouraged a fragmented system at national level, alongside centralization within policy networks;

3   Relations between different levels of government became entangled with processes of economic management by central government, which came to dominate over the initial bases for co-operation between them (i.e. the delivery of particular services);

4   The introduction of the new political agenda of Thatcherism also helped to undermine the old arrangements, as proposals for privatization challenged the assumptions of continued growth on which they were based – as Rhodes puts it: 'Party ideology has been the grit in the well-oiled machinery of the policy networks';

5   Because the policy networks are represented within the departments of central government as well as outside it, the policies of the centre were often characterized by confusion and uncertainty – the centre failed to speak with one voice;

6   Government actions helped to undermine the longer-term insulation of local and national policy elites from each other. Local élites were under challenge and responded with an increased politicization and readiness themselves to challenge the centre, instead of using the policy networks to negotiate;

7   The hierarchical 'command operating code' taken up by central government in this period was at variance with the differentiated polity (or form of political life) with which it had to deal. 'The command code,' says Rhodes, 'represents a failure to comprehend that British government is a multi-form maze of interdependence. To operate a code at variance with this reality is to build failure into the initial policy design.'

(This summary is based on Rhodes 1985, Section 4)

Although so far emphasis has been placed on the ways in which central government helped to upset the existing arrangements, and in a sense to reap the whirlwind which it sowed, it is also important to recognize not only that there were local factors helping to encourage 'territorial resistance' to pressures from the centre, but also that there were pressures from below which were encouraging local authorities to move in the opposite direction, particularly as they did not feel any substantial responsibility for national economic policy. Through most of the 1980s, with a Conservative government in power, the realities of electoral arithmetic tended to mean that few Conservative councils survived in urban areas, and even in the shires there was a dramatic rise in support for the Alliance parties in the mid-1980s, which left many councils under no overall control. The growth of three party politics in the 1980s, left Labour marginalized and irrelevant in some areas, but much stronger in others – in its traditional and more recent heartlands, in the urban authorities, inner London, the North of England, South Wales and Central Scotland (see Green 1987, pp. 203–4).

Labour came to power in several councils at a time of crisis in urban government, particularly in the inner cities and other older industrial areas. The selective impact of Britain's economic crisis left the inner cities with major concentrations of unemployment and devastated the country's industrial heartlands (see, for example, Robson 1988, ch. 1 and Martin 1988). Poverty, too, was increasingly concentrated in Labour controlled authorities. In most areas, housing stock left from the 1950s and 1960s was falling apart, in need of major repair and renovation (and sometimes demolition). In 1980/81 and then in 1985, major riots (or uprisings, see Gilroy 1987, pp. 236–44) took place in many of Britain's cities. Somehow local authorities had to respond to these problems with the increasingly limited resources at their disposal. Just at the time when the centre wanted to reduce spending, in many areas local authorities were faced with growing pressures to increase them.

Within policy networks it could be argued that there were identifiable centres, even if their interests were not always consistent with the stated ambitions of the 'centre' as defined by Prime Minister or Cabinet. But some of the new areas of policy development taken up by Labour and some Conservative councils in the early 1980s were still less susceptible to control from the centre, precisely because they were not statutorily based, and, were in effect, outside existing policy networks. This was particularly true of spending on economic development. Even in the 1970s, central government was concerned that spending in this area was taking directions which might not be in line with its priorities, and a committee was set up within the Department of the Environment to assess its importance, although the final report tended to minimize it (Burns 1980). (For a discussion of the growth of local economic development initiatives in the 1980s, see, for example, Campbell 1990.)

One of the difficulties associated with the local government system in Britain – at least for those trying to control or direct it from above – is that its institutional and legal arrangements appear to require the delegation of specific powers from above, but in practice what local governments do helps to determine what is possible (and legal). A great deal of the day-to-day activity of councils and their employees exists in the cracks within the system, which allow action to be taken, unless it is specifically prohibited. Local economic development activity has survived and developed since 1945 on the basis of a number of legislative silences rather than a series of clear powers. Some activities have drawn their legitimacy from planning legislation (for example, finding alternative premises for non-conforming uses, taking the general planning interests of an area into account), whilst others have been a consequence of housing legislation, as land for development has become available. Councils have often had, or taken, responsibility for managing their land holdings with a view to economic development (for example with powers under the Local Authorities (Land) Act 1963). Since the late 1970s, powers relating specifically to inner city development have been extensively used, and the definition of 'inner city' has often been a very wide one. And, of course, until the late 1980s Section 137 of the Local Government Act 1972 was used extensively to justify expenditure defined (by the council) as being in the interests of the residents of their area, even if it did not bring additional resources. Not until the Local Government and Housing Act 1989 were local authorities given explicit powers to spend money on economic development, and this new power was accompanied by equally explicit restrictions on what might be spent (and how it might be spent) as well as a requirement that councils undertaking such activities prepare local plans setting out what they intended to do (and to consult with the private sector).

Central–local relations in the 1980s (at least until the last years of the decade) did not appear to show a process of inexorable centralization, in which only one side could win. On the contrary for much of the decade there was a strong sense that a range of issues were under political contention whose outcome was uncertain (even if it was acknowledged that central government was likely to have the final say). This was a period in which new initiatives were being developed in local authorities up and down the country. There is no doubt that in the early 1980s, local authorities became more ideologically differentiated across the political spectrum, particularly in urban areas. There was a marked increase in 'party politicization' which was reflected in different ways in different places (Leach et al. 1986, p. 197, Gyford et al. 1989; see also Gyford's discussion of the rise of local socialism, Gyford 1985). No longer were disputes solely, or mainly, about which party might be better at administering a set of agreed services. The nature of the services themselves and their modes of delivery were genuine political issues at local level. Because of their key role in the development of the Keynesian welfare state through the post-war period, once the old certainties of social democracy began to be called into question – as they were in the context of economic problems through the 1970s – local authorities were increasingly forced to redefine their own positions as well.

Privatization, value for money and council house sales were the main issues for the right, whereas for the left, local authorities became a battleground for the defence and extension of collective provision. Liberal-controlled councils saw themselves as mapping out a 'third way' which combined financial constraint, responsiveness and closeness to consumers (e.g. through the decentralization policies of councils such as Tower Hamlets; see Hoggett 1991, pp. 253–4, Lowndes and Stoker 1992a and 1992b). Butcher et al. suggest that the responses of Conservative authorities to the heightened political temperature of the 1980s can be clustered into three main types: the contract authority, the enterprising authority and the business-corporatist authority. They emphasize that Conservative councils were not simply creatures of central government in this period. Using this typology, the 'contract authority' is defined as being committed to the delivery of existing services through the issuing of contracts to private or voluntary agencies. This type of authority is likely to seek to reduce costs by limiting services and will have little interest in notions of community: 'the link between the voter and the councillor will be confined to holding down expenditure and the level of the community charge'. The 'enterprising authority' is one which remains committed to notions of public service, but does not accept that this implies support for local state provision, instead seeking to work with voluntary and private sector agencies. Such an authority retains an interest in developing new services, rather than merely being a 'passive' provider of services, in part in order to attract new residents who see a role for municipal spending in sustaining the 'quality of life'. Finally, the 'business corporatist authority' is one which sees itself as serving the wider interest by developing closer relations with the business and commercial sectors. Such an authority might remain rooted in collectivism (and direct service provision) but its ambitions would be defined in terms of those with which it develops partnership arrangements (Butcher et al. 1990, pp. 161–5). Holliday's analysis of political change in Kent during the 1980s also suggests that some Conservatives were setting out to develop a new role for local government, which did not always fit very well with some of the proposals emanating from the centre (Holliday 1991a and b) (see Chapter 3).

It was a time when Thatcherite initiatives were being developed in some places, a time when what came to be called local socialism appeared to be on the agenda in others, and in which many councils were setting out more modestly to explore what was possible within the limits they faced. They were increasingly setting out to stretch those limits. There was continued evidence of new initiatives developing at local level (including, for example, the expansion of local economic development, the spread of decentralization policies and devolved management structures, a growing concern for equal opportunities, and more recently for 'green' issues). None of this suggested an area in decline, despite the defeat for the local authority left in campaigns over ratecapping in 1985–6 and the abolition of the GLC and the metropolitan counties in 1986.

One way of illustrating this may be to look briefly at the experience of the 'local socialist' councils at this time. Even in the late 1980s it was possible to argue, without stretching reality too far, that 'the alliance around radical labourism has changed the contours of local and national politics, it set the new left agenda of the 1980s' (Campbell 1987, p. 101). Local government seemed to have a greater political significance as a source of radical initiative than at any other time since 1945. Although it is dangerous to exaggerate the number of councils which identified with 'local socialism' in any active sense, since most Labour authorities continued to follow more orthodox approaches, it did nevertheless represent an attempt to launch a new political agenda from below, from within local government. Not all Labour councils moved to the left in this period, although most were influenced by ideas generally associated with the left of the Labour Party. In the early 1980s councils such as the Greater London Council, Hackney, Islington, Lambeth, Sheffield, South Yorkshire, Stirling and Walsall among others had reputations for being 'socialist'[3]. But it is misleading to imagine that there was any single ideology which can be labelled 'local socialism' or 'municipal socialism'. There was no identifiable municipal socialist programme being im-plemented up and down the country between 1981 and 1986. The differences of emphasis between the policies adopted by the different councils were often as striking as any ambitions which they shared.

It is nevertheless possible to identify similar policy developments across a range of councils at this time which deserve to be acknowledged (and this is reflected in a number of publications, including Blunkett and Jackson, 1987, Boddy and Fudge 1984a, Cochrane 1986b, Gyford 1985, Lansley et al. 1989, Green 1987 and Wainwright 1987 as well as more ephemeral texts, such as Labour Co-ordinating Committee 1981, 1984 and 1988). Gyford effectively sums up the position:

> The nature of this local socialism is best understood not in terms of a single coherent ideology but as a syndrome or a set of associated

characteristics. These characteristics would include: a concern for issues hitherto absent from or marginal to conventional local government, such as local economic planning, monitoring the police, women's rights, and racial equality; a disdain for many of the traditional ways of conducting local authority business; a view of local government as an arena both for combating the policies of a Conservative government and for displaying by example the potential of grass roots socialism; and, perhaps most fundamentally, a commitment to notions of mass politics based upon strategies of decentralization and/or political mobilization at the local level

(Gyford 1985, p. 18)

Three main features united the local socialist councils. First, their leaders wanted to present an effective alternative to the policies of the Conservative government. They wanted to show in practice that there was an alternative which worked. Where the Thatcher Government and the 'new right' stressed the role of the market, the left authorities stressed the value of state intervention − of collective rather than individual solutions. Secondly, they wanted to present an alternative to the experience of Labour in power in the 1970s. Many activists first developed their radicalism as part of the process of fighting cuts in service provision and financial support imposed by the Callaghan Government in the late 1970s. They rejected the corporatist policies which had involved the striking of bargains between union leaders, big business and the state behind closed doors, and stressed the need for wider democratic involvement and the political mobilization of ordinary people. Thirdly, they were committed to a path which valued local initiative in its own right, as an alternative model to centralization and the market, offering new opportunities for democratic control. Although they had few illusions about local government as it existed, many of the activists (whom Gyford labelled the 'new urban left') shared the ambitions of David Blunkett and Keith Jackson who emphasized:

the need to build democracy; since democracy is more than the mere right to cast a vote at elections. Active politics of this kind has commonly only been available to privileged élites and powerful interests. Local politics is about its extension so that people can run their own affairs, adopting an increasingly broad perspective as confidence in democracy grows

(Blunkett and Jackson 1987, p. 5)

By the end of the 1980s the local authority left were divided and in retreat. They had failed in their ambitions to challenge the Thatcher governments effectively and were, instead, involved in mutual recrimination and post mortems (see, for example, Lansley et al. 1989). But for a time at least they had succeeded in being stubbornly resistant to the agendas of central government and had confidently attempted to present alternatives, and to claim their own sources of democratic political legitimacy. Stoker suggests that by the end of the decade this group had effectively been replaced by a group he describes as 'urban managerialist' (rather than 'urban left') which shared some of the left's ambitions, but were distinguished from them by 'the more modest nature of their political agenda' (Stoker 1991a, p. 48).

NOT QUITE THE END

The failure of the policies developed for local government by central government in the 1980s can be explained in part by an apparent belief in the effectiveness of the hierarchical model of co-ordination at central level. The evidence suggests that some senior civil servants and leading national politicians may believe that they can determine what happens at local level by legislating for it. White papers tend to talk in terms of Britain as a 'unitary state' (for example Department of the Environment/ Welsh Office 1983, para. 1.2) and the frequency of legislative reform suggests that there is a belief that eventually it will be possible to construct the appropriate 'rational' structure of government. Unfortunately, the evidence of the 1970s and 1980s also suggests that such a belief is difficult to sustain in practice. Every change from above seems to have been met by adjustments elsewhere in the system first to take account of and then to evade the intended consequences of the central legislation. As we have already noted, even the attempts to reduce local government spending were much less successful than the political rhetoric on both sides would have suggested. If the relationship between central and local government is a hierarchical one, it is certainly a complex hierarchy. It looks rather more like a constant process of negotiation in which the ground rules are not always clear and may be changed by the centre with often unpredictable consequences. Rhodes' conclusions emphasize the 'messiness' of the process, suggesting that it will simply become increasingly difficult to understand who is accountable for what and to whom and to predict the outcomes of local and national political decisions (Rhodes 1985, 1991). It is easy to be sympathetic towards this view. It all certainly looks like a bit of a mess, and it is difficult to believe that it is quite what central government wanted to achieve at the beginning of the 1980s. The danger is, however, that one loses sight of broader processes of change in cataloguing detailed failures of implementation. As later chapters of the book will argue, it is possible to identify a general direction to the changes which have taken place, even if they are not all completely consistent, and even if they do not always fit very well with the stated intentions of politicians and civil servants.

The programme of the third Thatcher Government elected in 1987 was probably the most explicit in terms of its attempts to recognize and restructure Britain's local government system. No area of local government responsibility escaped scrutiny, with education and housing being the most obvious targets, compulsory competitive tendering being extended and yet another set of changes (in the form of the community charge) being introduced for the finance of local government. In response to these proposals Travers acknowledged that central government did not succeed in removing local autonomy in the 1980s, but suggested that the legislative programme of the late 1980s might be more successful (Travers 1989, pp. 19–20). Attention was also drawn to the apparent contrast between moves towards decentralization in other European countries and continued centralization in the UK (for example in Crouch and Marquand 1989). And some of those analysing the wider aspects of the reform programme suggested that it promised greater central control over a significant range of policy areas. After surveying the provisions of the Education Reform Act 1988, the Housing Act 1988, the Local Government Finance Act 1988 and the NHS and Community Care Act 1990, Glennerster et al. concluded that the most likely outcome was increased central power. 'As central departments lost their role in guiding an expanding welfare state, so they increased their role in controlling a static one' (Glennerster et al. 1991, p. 412). What has happened, they argued, was that local government had lost out with the creation of a series of 'small-scale semi-representative' bodies who were responsible directly to the centre. The authors suggested that these changes were the result of an unspoken and probably unholy alliance between civil servants wishing increased power and greater control over programme budgets and politicians wishing to undermine Labour controlled authorities (see also Dunleavy 1991, ch. 8). If this was the intention of the civil servants it is perhaps worth pointing out that their ambitions may be more difficult to achieve in practice. The problem may simply have been shifted to the management of other agencies, themselves resistant to pressure from above. Central government now has to manage housing associations, training agencies, schools and polytechnics (new universities) whose activities were previously embedded within elected local government. It is not yet clear that fragmenting these responsibilities and encouraging different forms of accountability has increased central control. Intuitively, at least, it seems possible that it may decrease the ability of the centre to control or manage its new creations – particularly as in most cases their legal position is more ambiguous because they straddle the public, private and voluntary sectors (utilizing Rhodes' language, in other words the policy networks may become more rather than less complicated and more difficult to manage from the centre).

Nevertheless it is difficult not to conclude that elected local government lost out substantially from these reforms. Yet they were not met with the same outcry as earlier legislative proposals that were supposedly a threat to autonomous local government. Following the logic of the arguments of the early 1980s, one might have expected this barrage of legislation to be met by commentaries which confirmed the end of local government. Instead, however, the emphasis seemed to shift towards noting opportunities and identifying new models for the future (in the form of an enabling authority or the search for more flexible and responsive delivery and managerial systems) (see, for example, Stewart and Stoker 1989b, particularly Part 1). It is almost as if the survival of local government in some recognizable form has so surprised the prophets of the early 1980s that they have had to do penance by trying to find a new role (and a future) for local government in the 1990s. Or it may just be that accepting the inevitability of continuing assault from above has encouraged them to look for acceptable survival mechanisms which then have to be justified as new opportunities. In the next two chapters we shall consider some of the ways in which attempts have been made to do this.

NOTES

1   This expenditure was that defined by the Department of the Environment as 'relevant' for the purpose of attracting rate support grant. In practice the actual expenditure of local government was always higher than this level (for example, because it included capital expenditure and some outlays not counted as 'relevant'), so the proportion of total spending covered by central government was always lower. The important point is, however, that whichever measure is used, the proportion of local spending funded by central government grant fell sharply in this period.

2   This is a net figure, after capital receipts are taken into account. Gross levels of capital spending rose by 65 per cent over the same period (Department of the Environment 1992, p. 10).

3   Although Liverpool is sometimes added to this list, the association of some of

its leaders with the Militant Tendency always made them reluctant to identify with a movement which seemed to emphasize the possibility of local solutions (see Taafe and Mulhearn 1988 for a sympathetic discussion of the Liverpool Labour Group's approach to local and national politics at this time).

Chapter Three

From state to market?

Few even of their strongest supporters would suggest that the Thatcher governments generated clear and unequivocal policies for local government. On the contrary, there has often been a high degree of confusion, because the government has been under competing rather than consistent pressures. Local government sometimes assumed a high political profile because it appeared to be an obstacle in the way of broader political change, rather than because it has always been a major focus of government attention in its own right. Often, policies for local government have simply been the consequence of following through the logic of other policies.

One ambition, for example, as we have seen, has been to control and reduce public sector (particularly welfare) spending, and an early target was spending at local level. This is, of course, one of the policies which led to all the accusations of centralization discussed in previous chapters. One sympathetic interpretation of this suggests that local governments were simply trespassing 'on the Government's economic space' (Bulpitt 1989, p. 70) and that financial controls were introduced to deal with this.

Another pressure, it has been suggested, was the desire to set boundaries for local political initiative, to stop challenges to what was defined as legitimate political power, expressed in the decision-making of national government. Mather explains the abolition of the GLC in terms of the Thatcher Government's 'reluctance to allow the policy agenda to be determined elsewhere' (Mather 1989, p. 214). Bulpitt argues plausibly that the politics of central–local relations in the 1980s can best be understood as a consequence of an unstable political compromise developed in the late 1930s and confirmed after 1945. This left local authorities to implement centrally agreed policies within a framework which also endorsed notions of local democracy, albeit on the (unspoken) assumption that there was little significant popular support for the institutions of local government. It was assumed that there would be no 'misbehaviour' at local level, but the economic and political pressures of the 1960s and 1970s made conflict more likely and the compromise could no longer be sustained (Bulpitt 1989, pp. 65–7). From this perspective it may be more appropriate to view centrally inspired 'attacks' on local government and local autonomy as attempts 'to get central–local relations back to the 1930s, when the two levels of government knew their respective places' (ibid., p. 73). Some of the conflicts between central and local government in the 1980s may also be explained simply by party political competition and the government's understandable desire to ensure that the country was safe for Conservatism.

THE MARKET AS SAVIOUR

But other ambitions are also apparent and suggest a different and more coherent vision for local government, in the context of a broader set of challenges to bureaucratic power made possible by the introduction of market measures or surrogates for them. The main thrust of the critique of local government which influenced the Thatcher Government was one which stressed the strength of market alternatives and the inherent weaknesses of bureaucratic (public sector) organization. Similar arguments were used to justify the privatization of the nationalized industries, to support the 'next step' initiatives within the Civil Service and the creation of relatively autonomous agencies such as the Benefits Agency, and to underpin the moves towards various kinds of health service trusts in the National Health Service (see, for example, Bartlett 1991, Ibbs 1988, Metcalfe and Richards 1990, ch. 11).

The argument of those who seek to introduce market mechanisms into the delivery of services currently provided through local government is clear enough. Its main focus is on the cleansing power of markets. It has two main elements. The first is the claim that it increases efficiency (with a dominant stress on 'value for money'), and the second that it increases direct accountability to 'consumers'. This approach implies a shift away from a view of local government as responsible to citizens (through political pressures and elections) towards one in which it is responsible to consumers (through forms of market pressure).

According to this argument, public service provision in local government operates 'in the interests of those who administer it', whereas private sector provision is more genuinely controlled by the public because it is 'dependent upon satisfying public taste' (Forsyth 1981, p. 1). This approach draws on arguments of public choice theorists (such as Niskanen 1971, 1973) who set out to explain the behaviour of 'bureaucrats' (in non-market situations) by utilizing the tools of economic theory which set out to analyse how 'rational actors' (seeking to 'maximize their utility') can be expected to behave in given situations (McLean 1987, p. 1). Because they do not sell their services in a market, bureaucrats cannot be profit-maximizers and so it is suggested that they seek to maximize their utility in other ways, in terms of extra power, prestige and status. As a result it is argued that budget holders in state bureaucracies will tend to maximize either their budgets, their staff or both, which is unlikely to lead to the most efficient form of service provision, since it will involve spending more money than is necessary to achieve a given level of service[1].

A further political consequence of this form of bureaucratic behaviour is that it will create groups dependent on and ready to campaign for increased spending. These groups may be territorially concentrated, thus reinforcing the position of some local politicians and bureaucrats, effectively making it possible to buy votes. Green has argued that 'the voices most strident in their demands for the "protection of public services" are those of the middle-class government salariat' who gain directly from it in terms of income, employment and status (Green 1985, p. 12). Others express concern about the 'disproportionate influence of pressure groups' focused on single issues, which make it more difficult to take account of the views of more 'amorphous' groups such as taxpayers and community charge payers (Pirie 1981, p. 11). Some also argue that the operation of the welfare system in this way tends to disadvantage the poor by generating a 'culture of poverty' and encouraging the growth of an 'underclass', dependent on welfare (Murray 1990). In effect it is suggested there may be an unholy alliance between the (state) professional middle classes, local (Labour) politicians and the poor to encourage high levels of spending which fail to deliver appropriate services or to assist those intended to benefit from support.

It is believed that moves towards market methods (or attempts to learn from the ways in which markets operate) will help to provide ways of challenging the power of professional interests and set up a different set of rules within which they may operate. Whilst it is recognized that a simple transfer to market methods will not be possible for all of the services provided by local government, it is argued that changes can be made which will represent moves in that direction: at least making it possible to move away from systems which give precisely the opposite messages to those which are appropriate or intended. Of course, the market view as expressed here is a normative one. The argument is that moves in this direction are necessary and should be taken. But, it is also clear that the strong assumption is that history is on the side of markets. Even where the market has not yet been successfully introduced into local government (perhaps because, as Pirie 1988 claims, it was at first politically necessary to compromise with powerful interest groups within organizations), it is suggested that market mechanisms will be increasingly important in the future. If state provision dominated in the post-war decades, now, it is suggested, is the time for markets to take over. Bureaucratic resistance may still exist, but its days are numbered.

Following the logic of this position it should be possible to break up local government service provision in ways which ensure either that it is effectively marketized (for example though privatization) or, more likely, some voucher system or similar system is developed to imitate market methods. More options need to be made available to ensure that local consumers can opt out of public sector provision (or, perhaps more accurately, buy into private or voluntary sector provision). Such a vision of the future implies a minimalist role for elected local government, responding to demand, but leaving other agencies to satisfy it. Minford argues strongly in favour of moves to 'de-politicize local government', suggesting that local authorities should be 'clubs providing services and charging for them according to the service's characteristics' (Minford 1988, p. 12). In areas where markets are likely to be weak, such as welfare provision, it is increasingly suggested that responsibility should be taken on by charitable or other voluntary organizations and that it might be possible to run local provision through a form of a locally-based community company (Adam Smith Institute 1989).

Some of these arguments seem to have found a more muted expression in the concept of an enabling authority, particularly as outlined by

Nicholas Ridley while Secretary of State for the Environment (Ridley 1988a). Emphasis is placed on enabling appropriate groups to do whatever is necessary, stressing the importance of competition. The intention is to encourage the growth of a much wider range of agencies capable of delivering services currently directly provided by local government. In some cases it may be that local government involvement is no longer required, but in general it is suggested that councils would retain a regulating and contracting role, with the expectation that they would pursue it 'fairly, efficiently and swiftly without stifling initiative and enterprise' (ibid., p. 29). Following this line of argument, Mather points to 'a more modest role as specifier, purchaser and regulator of community services,' (Mather 1989, p. 216) and goes on to argue that the business of councils could 'be despatched in one, two or three meetings a year' (ibid., p. 222).

This interpretation of the programme of the 'new right' in the Thatcherite 1980s has been developed by its supporters, and by those who wish to encourage further moves in the same direction. But the period has also been analysed in a similar way by writers with little sympathy for the strategy being adopted. Authors such as Gamble and Leys, for example, have suggested that a 'free market' and a strong central state fit well together, as long as the central state is under the control of convinced supporters of the free market, ready to resist attempts at political interference which may be generated at other levels of the system (for example, from the 'new urban left'). They stress the overall 'logic' of Thatcherism as a political project associated with neo-liberalism and the 'new right'. According to Gamble, 'the state must be minimal in its functions, but strong in carrying them out' and this implies the substantial undermining of potential sources of opposition, including local authorities (Gamble 1985, pp. 209–10; see also Leys 1989, pp. 344–55, and Gamble 1988). A move away from public provision towards market provision at local level would, of course, be consistent with this, confirming the '*de facto* abolition of local government' of which Leys warns (Leys 1989, p. 355).

THE EXPERIENCE OF MARKETS

The evidence of the 1980s about the extent to which market models have been successfully implemented is rather mixed. There has been a shift towards direct commercial (private or quasi-private sector) provision in some areas, such as public transport, where charging was already the norm. The municipal trading organizations of the past, with their separate accounts and budgets, have tended to move out of direct council control, while direct labour organizations have tended to move towards more separately identifiable accounts and rules on self-financing. In the field of housing, it has become increasingly difficult to subsidize the Housing Revenue Account from local tax income, and at the same time council houses have been transferred to the private market through sales to sitting tenants, and sometimes private developers or housing associations. The extent to which further existing council-based trading activities can be transferred directly to the private sector is probably limited, although the leisure industries may offer potential. Even council house sales seem to have reached saturation point and are no longer an issue of contention between the major political parties. The decline in council housing as a proportion of housing stock owes more to restrictions on new building than it does to sales of existing stock (Stoker 1988, pp. 181–2). Whilst the direct shifts to the private sector are clearly of some importance, because they confirm a renewed market emphasis, it is also important to note that they did not fundamentally challenge existing arrangements which already assumed market forms of provision, even if they were subsidized and organized through the local state.

The delivery of these services was already handled through forms which are recognizable as markets. But elsewhere the search for market measures has been more difficult. It is often a search for market surrogates rather than the creation of consumer-based markets. It is difficult to find an equivalent to the individual consumer within those parts of the welfare state where either that consumer cannot be expected to have the level of income adequately to express demand, or, perhaps, for example in the case of child protection, the 'consumer' is simply unable to express a clear preference. Stewart asks who the final consumer is in the case of education: the child, the parent, or the future employer? As he points out, 'There is no individual customer for smoke control or for environmental health. In the public sector law and order are enforced and the language of the customer barely fits the restaurateur being prosecuted, or the criminal being charged' (Stewart 1992, p. 29).

As a result, it is often more appropriate to use the term 'quasi-market', which suggests that it is not possible (even for neo-classical economists) to say at a theoretical level whether the mechanism works better or worse than other forms of bureaucratic organization – 'quasi-markets' are not necessarily more or less effective than other forms of bureaucratic allocation. They do not have the theoretical advantages of private markets expressing consumer preference which are suggested by some economic theories. It may nevertheless still be possible to use the market model as a guide or source of ideas. But it needs to be viewed rather differently, as a political option (frequently bureaucratically managed) rather than a universally objective guiding principle. The attempt is to generate rules which encourage desired behaviour by bureaucrats and professionals, as well as opening up previously closed areas of decision-making, policed by professionals, to the demands of those increasingly defined as consumers. It has been suggested that it is important 'not to take an a priori stand either for or against' quasi-markets. Instead the experiments generated by the Thatcher governments should be monitored 'to provide us with evidence as to whether, suitably adapted and extended, quasi-markets constitute the way forward for social policy' (Le Grand 1990, p. 14). This is a far cry from approaches which start with 'the market' as a universal model and then justify reforms in terms which simply appeal to this model.

The Education Reform Act 1988 seemed to move sharply towards market-style arrangements, giving schools the ability to manage their own budgets and making it possible for schools to opt out of local authority control (Ranson and Thomas 1989). The local management of schools (LMS) implies schools buying in a range of services and being allocated resources according to a formula based on pupil numbers, leaving effective managerial and professional control at the level of the school in the hands of their governors, headmasters and headmistresses. The opting out of schools – moving to grant maintained status – simply reinforces this, with funds being allocated directly from the Department of Education. At the same time it was hoped to create a network of specialist city technology colleges, jointly funded by central government and private sector sponsors.

In practice the consequences of these changes have been uncertain. The numbers of schools opting out of local authority control was not as great as the government had hoped, although it seems scheduled to rise in the wake of the Conservatives' election victory in 1992 (only 217 out of 25,000 had done so before then, but the Government has a – possibly over-optimistic – target of 4,000 in the next few years. Radley 1992, p. 29). But there is already some evidence of increased competition between schools, particularly in places such as London where pupils are able to cross borough boundaries. The level of competition for teachers and pupils is clear in the increase in advertising and glossy brochures now available. There are already fears that some schools will be closed through lack of demand and that some of those in demand (and many city technology colleges) are using their new positions to select pupils who they think will fit in best, relegating others to less popular schools.

Again, however, the nature of the market involved is uncertain, to say the least. The introduction of a national curriculum, for example, suggests that competition and choice will be limited by the imposition of common tasks across the board. And the power of professionals within the educational system to reinterpret the pressures from above should not be underestimated. Their role seems to have been crucial in resisting the introduction of voucher systems which could have been used as currency across the private and public sectors of education. The role of governors still varies significantly between schools, because of continuing tensions between governors and teaching professionals about who should run them (Deem et al. 1992, p. 211). At local level the development of networks between schools, whether linked through the local authority or following from the initiative of schools themselves, may also work against straightforward market models (Ranson and Thomas 1989, pp. 71–6).

The relatively high turnover of school governors suggests that headteachers are going to have a still more important role in the new system, so change may depend on the extent to which they take on the market-style values implied by the new arrangements. The market is substantially constrained by limitations on school numbers since schools cannot simply expand to meet demand, particularly since, at least for schools which have opted out, local education authorities remain responsible for the provision of buildings. The position of local government has certainly been substantially undermined. Education departments have in the past been the biggest spenders in local government (until recently accounting for 35 per cent of council spending in England) (Department of the Environment 1991a) and in practice have often existed as almost independent fiefdoms within the councils of which they are nominally part. The Education Reform Act has certainly made it difficult to sustain that, but the changes are difficult to explain as a clear cut move towards the market. As indicated in Chapter 1, some have suggested that the real explanation for the changes can more easily be explained in terms which stress the desire of civil servants within the Department of Education to regain power (and control over budgets) which was lost with the cuts of the mid-1970s (Glennerster et al. 1991, pp. 393–8).

The community care legislation (the National Health Service and Community Care Act 1990) gives local government prime responsibility for managing and co-ordinating community care provision at the centre of a wider network including health authorities, trusts, voluntary agencies and private sector organizations. The emphasis is on encouraging the development of a 'mixed economy of care'. The Griffiths Report (Griffiths 1988), on which the legislation is based, suggests that the existing role of social services departments in the field of community care should be split around the distinction between purchaser and provider. Purchasers will be those (with budgets) who develop packages of care for individuals on the basis of an assessment of their needs. Providers will be those who deliver the packages of care. The purchasers will become care managers (i.e. those who manage and develop packages of care and the work of others for individuals) while the providers have been described by the Audit Commission as community carers (Audit Commission 1986). In principle care managers are expected to become the purchasers of services provided by others, whether employed by the direct services parts of social services departments, by various forms of trust (including hospital trusts) and voluntary agencies, or by private sector organizations (for example, in the form of residential care). Except in a few specialist areas (such as child protection investigation) the provider role is increasingly defined as one in which non-professional skills will be most important and those employed will tend to be low paid and work part time. Emphasis will be placed on informal care (usually provided by mothers, sisters, daughters or wives for little or no payment) and voluntary work, as well as support from care assistants and home helps.

Despite the market-influenced language and the stress on encouraging the use of agencies outside the public sector, this is a 'mixed economy' with so much state regulation and involvement that it is hard to see it in market terms. Local authorities have a responsibility (in consultation with the National Health Service and the voluntary and private sectors) to prepare and publish community care plans which set out the ways in which they expect services to develop and need to be agreed with central government. The legislation assumes the creation of an extensive network of inter-agency working and joint planning in which public sector agencies are required to take the lead. Paradoxically in a period of centralization, it is perhaps also worth noting that the Act implies the return of a responsibility to local government which was lost long ago, since local authorities will become responsible for the provision of financial support to those entering residential care in the private or voluntary sectors.

Probably the most obvious way in which market methods have been imposed by central on local government has been in legislation requiring the privatization of specified aspects of their work and the awarding of contracts for these services to other agencies through a process of compulsory competitive tendering (CCT). The main emphasis of CCT has been in areas of straightforward service delivery (such as refuse disposal and housing maintenance) or ancillary work (such as cleaning within council-owned buildings). Although there has been a growth in private companies providing services in this area, in-house direct labour organizations have also frequently remained competitive. Most privatization involves the contracting out of services rather than their direct provision for payment by 'customers', and, according to a report on the first rounds of CCT, monitoring is still based mainly on responding to customer complaints and inspection by council officers (LACSAB 1990). Maybe that is as much as could be expected, and it suggests the importation of methods of financial and management control from the private sector, developing the notion of 'value for money' which has been encouraged by the Audit Commission as well as government ministers and finance professionals. But that also suggests that the implications of the changes have not been as significant as some hoped and others feared. The local authority itself either remains the final consumer or, in its role as monitor and regulator, acts as surrogate for the final consumer. Such contracting out has, in any case, not been restricted to local government (or indeed the public sector) but has also been marked in the private sector, where major corporations have contracted out much activity which is not seen as one of their core activities. In her wider analysis of the growth in self employment, for example, Hakim stresses the importance of this form of sub-contracting, both to the self employed and to large companies in the private sector (Hakim 1988, p. 444). So the changes in local government can hardly be explained solely in terms which stress the inefficiencies of public provision, or a move to marketization. They need to be placed in the context of more general changes (see Chapters 5 and 6).

Within local government the moves towards privatization via contracting out have also been accompanied by an increase in the numbers of white-collar (core) staff, which seems to undermine arguments which suggest that the role of local government is becoming more modest. It looks more like a way to increase labour discipline than to extend the market. In some cases it may, as Dunleavy suggests, simply offer a way for the chief officers to undermine the position of a troublesome set of blue-collar subordinates (Dunleavy 1986, p. 21). Evidence from the first rounds of compulsory competitive tendering suggests that between 61 per cent (in building cleaning) and 97 per cent (in catering for education and welfare) of contracts have been awarded to councils' own direct service organizations, with a higher proportion of higher value contracts also being awarded to those organizations (LACSAB 1990. See also Painter 1991a).

It is not clear that privatization of this type – based on the issuing of contracts – necessarily encourages 'free' competition. On the contrary, there is also some evidence that, in the short term at least, it may encourage close sets of relationships between favoured suppliers and particular local governments. Perhaps not surprisingly, the boards of many firms competing for local government contracts are peppered with directors with local government experience. The importance of personal linkages is probably greater at local level, where for example, management buy-outs are usually accompanied by guaranteed orders for some time, and, of course, the specialist local expertise (particularly in white collar areas) makes it difficult for outsiders to compete. An extreme example of this process came to light in West Wiltshire in the early 1990s, when allegations of corruption over a privatized computer software company led to formal criminal investigation, but it is possible to develop close links without overstepping the bounds of legality.

This can be illustrated with the example of some of the new town development corporations (Telford, Milton Keynes and Warrington/ Runcorn) in which the process of contracting out white-collar work started earlier. Work was simply carried on by the same people on new (guaranteed) contracts which allow the agencies to undercut existing private sector agencies for other orders. In a carefully worded report the National Audit Office has expressed concerns about the ways in which a number of new town corporations ostensibly privatized many of their professional activities, while, in effect, issuing contracts to their previous employees (Comptroller and Auditor General 1990). The justification for moving in this direction was that the development corporations were in danger of losing the specialist expertise of their staff because they were coming to the end of their lives and when staff left they would be difficult to replace. If instead they were employed in 'business ventures' they might have more security of employment, would be able to build up a wider clientele and would not be restricted by public sector pay scales. The report suggests that there was insufficient oversight from the Department of the Environment and that the lack of competition for contracts may have led the corporations to pay more than was necessary (although lack of detailed figures makes the report's authors reluctant to draw definite conclusions on this matter (see p. 22).

So far emphasis has been placed on the way in which locally-based arrangements might work against contracting out as a market option, but in the longer term the level of private sector bidding for contracts is likely to increase. Some of the possible consequences of this are discussed in the next chapter, but it is worth noting at this stage that it may be misleading to assume that a multiplicity of relatively small enterprises will bid for contracts so that councils can choose between them relatively easily. On the contrary it is apparent that some service areas are already dominated by a small number of large (sometimes multinational) concerns. One company owned one third of the contract cleaning market in Britain in 1988 and mergers have continued since then absorbing smaller enterprises (see Allen 1988, p. 126; see also Ascher 1987, chs 3 and 7). The implication of this is that these organizations may become more powerful in negotiation than the councils with whom they are dealing and by whom they are being contracted. They may be able to set the conditions. In a discussion of the role of the major private sector utilities and local government in France, Lorrain highlights the danger that 'a group on the lookout for opportunities inevitably finds many occasions to serve its own interests as a first priority' (Lorrain 1991, p. 106). It is difficult effectively to monitor everything that such major organizations are doing.

THE CASE OF THE 'POLL TAX'

The introduction of the community charge (or poll tax) in the late 1980s can be understood as part of the continuing campaign to gain control over local decision-makers, at least in financial terms. But it was also justified as part of a broader shift to market mechanisms (see HMSO 1986). In principle, the matter must have seemed a relatively easy one to resolve. After all, domestic rates – paid by private households – were always an unpopular tax (particularly among Conservative supporters). The property values on which they were based were outdated, which meant that people living in recently valued (suburban) houses tended to pay rather more than those in older property. Calculating rental values when there was no private rental market for most of the properties being valued seemed increasingly peculiar. Complicated systems of rebates were necessary to make the rates workable (and fairer to those with low incomes living in highly valued property). Without rebates, the rates would have been highly regressive. Yet, there was also a widely held (although inaccurate) belief that council tenants did not pay rates at all, so that they were often seen as a particularly iniquitous tax on the middle class (and, if government propaganda was to be believed, particularly on widows). Wholesale revaluation might have been an option, but was tried in Scotland with such disastrous consequences (in terms of opposition from business as well as domestic ratepayers) that it merely confirmed the need to introduce some more extensive reform as soon as possible (in Scotland's case through the Abolition of Domestic Rates (Scotland) Act 1987). Anything, it appeared, must be better than the rates.

The basic principles of the poll tax were that each resident of the UK (outside Northern Ireland) over the age of 18 was expected to pay a flat rate charge set by her/his local authority to cover the costs of local services over and above those met by grant from central government (in the case of England and Wales including centrally collected income from business rates), income from charges for particular services (such as leisure services, fees for planning applications, etc.), and (in Scotland) non-domestic (i.e. locally collected business) rates. Concessionary levels were available for some categories of resident (such as students and those dependent on income support) but in principle everybody (with a few exceptions such as prisoners, monks and nuns) was expected to make *some* payment (at least 20 per cent of the charge level).

The poll tax seemed to offer ways of solving a number of political (and economic) problems. Above all, it appeared to offer the miraculous possibility of reducing levels of local government spending, while blaming rising costs (and high levels of local taxation) on 'profligate' (usually Labour) authorities. The other element in the package (in England and Wales) – the move from locally charged to nationally levied business rates – was explicitly directed towards undermining the ability of left-wing Labour councils – in London particularly – to fund their activities from taxes paid by business, instead of taxes paid by individuals (and voters). It was argued that the existing system meant that voters could escape the financial consequences of their (voting) decisions on levels of spending. They received benefits for which they did not have to pay. The poll tax was supposed to ensure that there was a direct link between local taxation and levels of spending by local government. If spending went up, so taxes would also rise and all voters would be affected, and would express their concerns through the ballot box. Everybody had to pay it, so that nobody could expect to receive services for which they had not made some financial contribution.

It was this that gave the tax its rather unconvincing official title of community charge, which never gained the acceptability of popular usage. Following the dominant government model, which suggested that everything could be translated into the language of markets, it was argued that the poll tax was somehow not a tax at all, but a fee levied for joint services provided to individuals at local level. It was in other words a charge, not a tax. And, of course, it was a *community* charge because . . . well, because everybody knows that communities are 'good things' and it seems reasonable to pay for their upkeep.

The official name of the tax was intended to highlight the notion that residents were paying for a package of services supplied by or organized through the council. In principle consumers were expected to be able to judge whether the cost of the package they received was appropriate and to express their judgement, not by moving to places where the charge was lower, as some market theorists have suggested in the past, but by electing a council likely to manage the delivery of an appropriate package more efficiently. A closer relationship between what people paid in taxation and what was spent by their councils was supposed to make those councils more directly accountable to the electors (and, incidentally, to encourage electors to participate at local level).

Supporters of the legislation argued that:

> Every voter, now faced with paying their share of council expenditure will have a powerful incentive to consider the possible costs of their candidate's policies before they cast their vote. Officials will have to take account of the effect of their recommendations on the public they deal with. Councillors will have to consider the impact of their decision on their voters. Accountability and responsibility will reappear in many communities where, in recent years, both have been lamentably lacking . . . and this will create significant, and probably substantial, electoral and demographic pressure on authorities to reduce their expenditure.
>
> *(The Adam Smith Institute, 1989)*

The introduction of the poll tax in the late 1980s was part of the continuing campaign by central government to gain control over local decision-makers, at least in financial terms. Because the services were delivered at local level it was believed that it would be relatively easy for voter/consumers to compare the records of their own councils with those of their neighbours, and to draw the necessary conclusions. To assist in drawing these conclusions, not only did Conservative party political broadcasts frequently focus on differences between households on either side of local authority boundaries (one particular street which was the boundary between Conservative-controlled Wandsworth and Labour-controlled Lambeth was given regular attention in Conservative broadcasts for a time), but also it was hoped that the work of the Audit Commission (set up in 1983) would highlight differences between responsible and irresponsible councils. One of the Commission's functions was to investigate the delivery of services by councils, drawing attention to the differences in the 'economy, efficiency and effectiveness' with which they delivered them. With the help of such comparisons, it was hoped that the right judgements would be made by local electors, since they would be faced with clear-cut market incentives in the form of the promise of lower poll tax levels if they voted the right way. The pressures from above would also be reinforced by electoral pressures from below. It was, of course, assumed that the judgements made at local level would increasingly parallel those being made by the Conservative Government.

With hindsight it is all too easy to see the flaws in this vision (see also Gibson 1990). Some of them are listed below:

1 Most obviously, perhaps, the notion of a flat rate charge was from the start viewed as being highly unfair. The view that the rich and the poor (or the nearly poor) should pay the same, and that even those receiving subsistence payments through income support should pay something out of their meagre income, was not one with enough support to provide the basis for a new system of taxation. On the contrary this was one of the features which made the tax highly unpopular, and difficult to implement. And many of the poor really did face reductions in their income levels as a result of the poll tax. Despite some protection from the rebate system, nearly a third of those families with incomes in the bottom 20 per cent of the population lost out, while 22 per cent of those in the top 20 per cent made gains (Ridge and Smith 1991, Table 6.1). It was difficult not to believe that this was a strange basis on which to fund local welfare services, which are in part at least oriented towards providing support for the more vulnerable in our society. Households containing more than three adults were, of course, affected particularly seriously by the tax with two-thirds losing out, and young people facing particular problems. Although the tax was formally levied on individuals, members of households were 'jointly and severally' responsible, which meant that, in effect, parents were expected to police the payments of their children, or to make the payment themselves.

2 Imposing a flat rate charge on individuals and ensuring that it is levied as a lump sum (although generally payable in monthly instalments) certainly made the tax more obvious, but also helped to make it very inflexible. The charge was always going to look high because of this. It may be that this was the intention of the government, as long as the blame for the level set could be placed unequivocally on the council concerned. Since, however – with a few well publicized exceptions at top and bottom – the increases in charge levels across the country were far more similar than might have been expected, it was difficult to shift the blame in this way. On the contrary, the blame generally seems to have been firmly placed on central government. More

important, perhaps, for the principles underlying the tax, its visibility made it difficult to see how it could be used to pay for a high proportion of local spending. Yet if it could not be used in this way, it was difficult to see how the aim of electoral accountability could be fully achieved, since grants and other support from the centre would still dominate local authority budgets.

3 In practice the tax did not bring the promised shift to local responsibility. In fact it was accompanied by moves towards greater central control of local authority finance. The charge itself only raised a small element of the overall costs of local government – in England and Wales, the legislation which introduced the poll tax also effectively left central government responsible for a significantly increased proportion of local government finance because the uniform business (non-domestic) rate was now distributed from the centre, with the level also being determined centrally. Attempts to overcome the unpopularity of the tax by increasing grants from central government (for example, for transitional relief) reached their height in the 1991 Budget, which increased VAT by 2.5 per cent to pay a higher proportion of the costs of local government. Less than 20 per cent of these costs are now covered by local taxation. In other words, the general direction of change since the late 1970s was simply reversed in a way which seemed to undermine the case for the tax (projections for the yield of the council tax, introduced to replace the poll tax from 1993, suggest that there will be little change in this respect). Central government also retained the 'residual' power to cap the spending levels of individual local authorities and then explicitly took the power to cap charge levels, too. Since its inception, the set of arrangements surrounding the poll tax (with different forms of transitional relief) and the grant regimes which underpin it made it difficult to see any clear relationship between levels of local tax and levels of local spending. On the contrary, these seemed to owe rather more to national decisions about what was to count towards the SSAs of different councils. In effect the new arrangements made it substantially more difficult for local authorities to make local decisions on levels of spending, which might then be judged by their electors. A cynic might argue that the value of electing a local government under the same control as the party in national government lay not so much in the local policies which resulted, but in the more favourable financing likely to be available from the centre (see also Midwinter 1989 which draws on the Scottish experience where the failure of the tax was probably still more marked than in England and Wales).

4   The interaction between grant levels, spending and poll tax had painful consequences for local government. As we have seen, the proportion of local authority spending directly controlled by the centre actually rose significantly, but the pressures on the residual taxation still collected locally also increased sharply. In part, this was simply the result of the grant settlements made in the late 1980s. It seems as if the politicians believed their own propaganda, and felt that the introduction of the new tax should provide the opportunity to improve 'efficiency' and effect financial and service cuts. Since this view was not shared at local level, in England and Wales the change was instead met with decisions to set charges at levels (around one-third higher than those suggested by the government) which implied a real rise in local domestic taxation revenues of 22 per cent. As a result, as Ridge and Smith (1991) note in a report for the Institute of Fiscal Studies, the number of people paying more in real terms rose dramatically, with losers outnumbering gainers by three to one. Those who ended up paying most for the poll tax were precisely those on middle incomes (with no possibility of rebates) who might have been expected to support it most enthusiastically. Even if councils are not capped, the local taxes implied by additional spending above SSA are bound to be high, since they have to be funded solely from the poll tax (and now the council tax) because they attract no additional grant from the centre. This results in the 'gearing' effect, which means that an apparently small increase in total spending requires a disproportionately high percentage increase in the poll tax (Bailey 1991, p. 896). Small differences between council spending and government estimates lead to big variations in the tax levied. This is both misleading, in that it tells us little about policy differences between councils, and problematic for central government since it makes it likely that local tax levels will always be substantially higher than predicted by them.

5   Another aspect of the poll tax which received a great deal of attention was the high cost of collection associated with it. Because it required the construction of a separate register of those liable to pay it, and the need to keep the register up to date, it cost a great deal more to collect than the old system (estimates vary, but the Audit Commission has suggested that they more than doubled, rising from £5 to £12 a head. Audit Commission 1990). In other words, despite the stress on market measures, little attention was paid to the costs of the new system (or the value for money it represented). Equally important, perhaps, despite the high costs, simply collecting the poll tax also

proved much more difficult than anticipated. It was not easy to keep an accurate record in places where there is a constantly changing population. In London levels of turnover were around 50 per cent and significantly higher in some boroughs. Nor, given the tax's unpopularity, was it easy to make residents pay. Despite all the efforts of national and local politicians (Labour as well as Conservative), it proved difficult to generate much guilt about non-payment. Levels of non-payment were as high as 20 per cent in some places, with the average in England and Wales in the first year being around 6 per cent. In Scotland levels of non-payment were closer to 13 per cent in the first year and 20 per cent in the second year. The legal problems of poll tax collection have filled the newspapers over the past few years, as courts have faced major backlogs of cases, and have judged that computer records are unacceptable as evidence. Underpayment tended to be more of a problem precisely in those places which were in greatest need of spending, but also have residents whose incomes had been hit hardest by the tax and by the economic recession.

6   It is difficult to identify the precise packages provided in different places, distinguishing between what is provided by various agencies at local level. It is often difficult to distinguish between what is provided by different levels of government, not only distinguishing between district and county or regional levels, but also between local and central government. Although a survey carried out for the Widdicombe Committee in the mid-1980s found that most people were able to identify which councils were responsible for which broad category of service, there were still 20 per cent who were unaware which agency was responsible for street cleaning, 33 per cent who did not know which council was responsible for education and 55 per cent who did not know which council was responsible for home helps (Young 1986, Table 2.8). Similarly, although most of those interviewed were able to allocate responsibilities reasonably well between agencies, 59 per cent of those interviewed thought that hospitals, 27 per cent that electricity supply, and 28 per cent that the payment of unemployment benefit were local government responsibilities (Young 1986, pp. 30–31). If services are broken down rather more it becomes still more difficult (even for the best informed citizen) to make any clear judgements about which services provided by voluntary (or private) agencies receive support from which range of statutory and non-statutory (even private sector) bodies. This problem has been exacerbated, instead of being eased, by recent changes, which have begun to move the funding of some responsibilities from local to

central government. The most obvious of these include the funding of grant maintained schools, the channeling of finance for training through Training and Enterprise Councils and the incorporation of further and adult education colleges. It is ironic that a series of reforms which were initially intended to increase local electoral accountability, now seem to be moving responsibility away from the electoral arena and any hope of direct electoral accountability.

7   The arguments behind the poll tax substantially underestimated the welfare element of local government, which is such an important part of its activities. Not everybody benefits from all parts of local government, so that it is not clear what services each is paying for. Certainly they are not only paying for services from which they benefit. It is difficult to know quite how a childless person should assess the contribution she or he should make to the education system, or how young people should judge the share of the charge used to support the old. This does not mean, of course, that people are not prepared to pay for these services, but it calls into question the principle that they are making choices as consumers between packages of services they receive.

8   The strongest proponents of the poll tax seemed to underestimate the continued significance of local politics as a legitimating and representative process – the extent to which local government was still perceived as government. They took the view that the delivery of an agreed package of services was a relatively straightforward process which some did better than others, so that the key issue was to identify who did it best and make sure that they continued to do so. But there is little doubt that some of the reasons for differences between spending by councils are the result of political differences. Indeed, even some of the differences in 'efficiency' may also reflect differences in political priorities, since those who make the judgements of necessity also make decisions about what areas of spending are acceptable or unacceptable. The best known controversies have tended to focus on units concerned with issues of equal opportunities, with race issues, women's issues, or gay and lesbian issues. But these are not the most significant in explaining differences in spending, which are likely instead to reflect different attitudes to core responsibilities, such as education, housing and social services. An example of this might be the way in which some councils have allowed tenants to run up large rent arrears. The criticisms of this practice frequently made by the Audit Commission tend to miss the point, because they simply explain it in terms of more or less efficiency in debt collection,

when for some councillors, at least, it may be a matter of political principle not to put pressure on those they feel are unable to pay. One result of underestimating the importance of local politics has been that the government has found it difficult to explain why apparently high spending (and high taxing) councils have continued to be supported in local elections. Despite the high hopes of ministers, the poll tax did not turn local electors into agents for a Conservative central government. Indeed one more noticeable effect seems to have been to encourage the growth of a wider movement focused on resistance to the poll tax and its payment (see, for example, Bagguley 1992; Burns 1992).

Some core elements in the market-based (new right) agenda for change in local government have proved impossible to implement successfully. The case of the poll tax highlights this failure particularly clearly. It was the 'flagship' of the 1987 Conservative Government's programme but its unpopularity contributed substantially to the pressures which led to the replacement of Margaret Thatcher as Prime Minister and leader of the Conservative Party at the end of 1990. Its replacement with the council tax under John Major not only implies a move back towards a property tax like the rates (rather than a fictional charge for services received) but confirms a substantial shift towards direct central government grant funding of local authority services which makes the individual choice of voter/consumers at local level still more irrelevant than in the past.

CONCLUSION

There is certainly important evidence that market theories have influenced the direction of change at local level. But the influence has had ambiguous results. Much of the evidence suggests a stronger role for core elites within local government, both officers and councillors, rather than their replacement by an effective system of consumer choice. Dunleavy convincingly outlines some of the ways in which bureaucrats may seek to insulate themselves from public scrutiny, and retain budgetary control, while giving up direct delivery systems to other agencies (Dunleavy 1985, 1986). Some chief officers have certainly used the new stress on 'customer care' to argue against member involvement in policy-making (see, for example, Smith 1989, who sharply criticizes 'member influenced housing policies' in inner London, p. 2). The market model is not so much an assessment of what has happened but of what some people would still like to happen, particularly those on the more 'liberal' wing of the new right (see, for example, King 1989, pp. 195–7). Other changes need to be explained – for example, the growth of non-elected local government and partnerships with a significant direct input from business, the continued strength of central government, the continued (and sometimes success-ful) resistance to some of the changes from the professionals, as well as the left, in local government, and the alternative vision of some on the right at local level. The market vision may survive and come to dominate – no doubt in principle far more could be delivered along market lines – but at present the prospect of its success remains an open question. Looking to the market does not provide easy solutions to the problems of running the local welfare state. At best the market can be seen as a symbol around which change may be organized through (at best) 'quasi-markets' or bureaucratically managed markets. But that leaves open the important question with which the proponents of the market started out, namely who manages these markets and for whose benefit?

NOTES

1   Dunleavy has developed a more sophisticated model which utilizes public (or rational) choice theories to explain behaviour in public bureaucracies. He argues for a more complex (bureau-shaping) approach which acknowledges that agencies are not simply run by one bureaucrat at the top (so there may be processes of interaction within agencies as well as between them and between bureaucrats below the top level across agencies); that the costs to an individual bureaucrat of arguing for an increased budget also have to be considered; and that bureaucrats within organizations are not just concerned with one budget (he identifies at least four types of budget in which bureaucrats might have an interest and suggests that they are likely to view each of them differently). These ideas are developed extensively in Dunleavy 1991. They did not significantly influence the restructuring of local government in the 1980s (perhaps they should have done), but are helpful in highlighting the need to look more closely at processes of bureaucratic politics.

Chapter Four

Towards the 'enabling' authority?

The notion of the 'enabling' authority was, as we have seen, initially raised in the context of debates about ways of introducing market-based approaches to the delivery of local services. In principle it was suggested the main role of an elected local authority might simply be to issue contracts to other agencies and let them (enable them to) get on with it. Even within the formulation developed by Ridley, however, it was possible to identify new opportunities. 'Authorities,' he argued, 'will need to operate in a more pluralist way than in the past, alongside a wide variety of public, private and voluntary agencies. It will be their task to stimulate and assist these other agencies to play their part instead of, or as well as, making provision themselves' (Ridley 1988a, p. 8). Building on this, it has been strongly argued that, despite some of the rhetoric, it is a mistake to identify the Thatcherite vision for local government solely in terms which emphasize the move towards the market or towards centralization. Instead, it is suggested, it is important to stress new possibilities within that vision. Even the Audit Commission's stress on understanding 'customers' (rather than 'clients') needs to be interpreted as a challenge, rather than simply a call to opt out of responsibility through privatization (Audit Commission 1988). According to this argument, the 'enabling' authority needs to be reconsidered as one which implies a continued significant role for elected councils and their staff as developers of strategy, partners with other agencies and in monitoring the operation and form of sub-contracted services. The Audit Commission itself went on to emphasize this interpretation, suggesting that councils needed to reinterpret their role as being to encourage a diversity of provision from a range of agencies, rather than seeking to deliver them directly (Audit Commission 1989a).

LOOKING FOR THE ENABLING AUTHORITY

Brooke sets out to develop this notion most fully (Brooke 1989a and 1989b). He acknowledges the extent to which there has been a separation of service functions from local government, but sees this as offering the prospect of developing a wider vision at local level, making it possible for councils to comment and intervene more widely on issues of interest to their areas than has been the case in the past. He argues that a reduction in direct responsibilities for service provision will allow councillors more time 'to devote to more general concerns . . . They – or their visionary successors – will have as a main concern the overall welfare of their area. They will seek practical ways of influencing other agencies to achieve a desirable result. Enabling, in other words ensuring local choice, will be the main theme. As a concept this covers a range from job creation to services to the handicapped. There is no choice without an available job; no choice if access is impossible' (Brooke 1989b, p. 10). His vision of the future is one which celebrates fragmentation and the development of a range of single service agencies, but only on the basis that there remains a strong and coherent central political/professional/managerial leadership, based around 'a central core of strategic planners and regulators . . . Such a core would of necessity embrace officers of different professional disciplines. A second cadre of managerially inclined or entrepreneurial officers will run services either as independent agencies, private sector companies, voluntary bodies or direct service organizations' (Brooke 1989a, p. 60).

In some ways, this vision is not too dissimilar to the overall ambitions of the corporate planners of the 1960s and early 1970s. The Bains Report came to similar conclusions (see Chapter 1). But today the management of change is to be achieved through the issuing of contracts and the allocation of budgets instead of the appointment of chief executives and

the setting up of management teams and policy and resources committees, and it is set within a rather harsher financial and political
environment. Brooke is quite explicit about this, arguing that the
fragmentation of organizational responsibility in the 1980s and into the
1990s may paradoxically mean that there is increased pressure for
multi-disciplinary work and extensive collaboration between agencies.
But, he concludes, this also implies the need for conscious co-ordination
and strategic thinking, which can best be carried out through an 'enabling'
authority (Brooke 1989b, pp. 8–9). For him it is the local authority above
all which has the potential to bring 'order to chaos' (ibid., ch. 3).

This vision can be made to fit in with, and indeed to follow from, the
overall programme of the Thatcher Government, at least as reinterpreted
by senior professionals within local government, although it contrasts
sharply with some of the more market-oriented rhetoric discussed in the
last chapter. Brooke himself sees it as being consistent with the aspirations
of the left as well as the right of the political spectrum. The aims of the
different political parties may be different, but, he argues, whatever they
are, opportunities exist to develop them within an enabling authority.
Strategic managers within local government would be able to work with
whatever party was in control of the council.

Others more directly in sympathy with the neo-liberal project have
developed arguments whose implications locate the enabling authority
more directly within their own programme. At a symposium organized
by the Institute of Economic Affairs, for example, King argued strongly
against political centralization, and for the allocation of additional powers
to local government – particularly powers of legal regulation rather than
additional service responsibilities. His suggestions include the possibility
of local rules on matters such as levels of alcohol acceptable in breath tests,
controls on litter and urban congestion (including forms of charging), and
locally-based distribution of vouchers for education and the health service
(which might also be organized on a more local basis). Although he
emphasized that his suggestions were ideas for consideration, rather than
finally formulated proposals, King's model is clearly one which implies a
continuing if rather different role for local government as an enabling
authority (although he does not use that term). His is a strong plea against
a central government monopoly on power, and for local autonomy to
allow experimentation at a local level on initiatives which may be
developed at a later stage, to act as a brake on central initiatives (not only is
he not sanguine about the possibility of a permanent free market majority
at national level, but he also suggests that strong central government is
likely, whatever the political party in control, to encourage a growth of

bureaucratic power and irrational decision-making), and to allow for a comparison between a series of governments at local level. Unless those local governments have a high degree of discretion, he suggests, comparison between them will be worthless (King 1988, p. 7; see also the analysis of decentralization in France developed by Salmon 1987 for similar arguments). King goes so far as to affirm that devolved tax power is 'good for economic performance' (King 1988, p. 8) and even to suggest that a local business tax may be appropriate to reflect different levels of service available in different places (ibid., p. 12). Few of the more traditional and beleaguered defenders of local government (academics or practitioners) would dare to make similar claims, which suggests that matters are by no means settled, even among neo-liberals.

Holliday takes a rather different view of the rise of the enabling authority, suggesting that it can also be understood as the product of locally-based pressures, reflected in the rise of what he calls the 'new suburban right'. He argues that this group, members of which are now in control in a number of authorities (such as Kent, on which he focuses), are committed to an interpretation of local politics which stresses the importance of strategic decision-making and plays down the politics of service provision. He suggests that the concept of the enabling authority is part of a broader 'local Conservative vision of the proper place and shape of local government' (Holliday 1991b, p. 54). This vision, he argues, is one which is 'genuinely governmental' precisely because it does not see itself simply as part of an administrative system delivering welfare and other services. In the case of Kent this understanding made it possible for the council to take an active part in developing a range of economic policies and has led the council to develop a Transfrontier Development Programme (creating a Euroregion) with the French region of Nord-Pas de Calais in order to gain access to European Community funds. Holliday contrasts this approach with that of more traditional Conservative authorities and with the Audit Commission's interpretation of the 'competitive council' which sees local authorities as non-political service providers (see Chapter 2). He draws more fully on arguments developed by Ridley to justify his interpretation of the enabling authority as a legitimate one for a Conservative council, stressing the importance of local government having a political role, i.e. acting as *government* rather than administration. Ridley called on local government to follow central government's route: 'Central government has divested itself of activities which it was never well equipped to discharge, and concentrated on taking political decisions. That process must spread to local government too' (Ridley 1988b quoted in Holliday 1991b, p. 58). 'The logic of NSR thinking,' argues Holliday, 'is to institute a local government system in which the competitive council, in its pluralistic local environment, acts as the political will of the local community' (Holliday 1991b, p. 59).

The alliance between local politicians and the new strategic managers is clearly important in developing the notion of the 'enabling authority' whether as it is seen by Brooke or in the rather different interpretation by Holliday. Holliday recognizes this in his discussion of change in Kent during the 1980s, where a new council leader (elected in 1984) and a new chief executive (appointed in 1986) played a major part in achieving and directing change, although they built on changes which had been taking place since the mid-1970s. Holliday describes the changes as a 'structural and managerial revolution' and a 'cultural revolution' (Holliday 1991a, p. 444; see also Young and Hadley 1990, which confirms the importance of the management style of the Director of Social Services in attempting to transform existing arrangements in the neighbouring county of East Sussex).

But the idea of an enabling authority can also be reinterpreted in ways which do not accept the underlying premises of the Thatcher Government and its supporters (even as reinterpreted by the 'new suburban right'), suggesting that the market is not always the best way to determine the allocation of resources or the provision of services, and arguing that the notion of an enabling authority should not just be the property of Conservatism at national or local level. Instead it may be possible to identify ways in which the new rules can be used to construct a more co-operative or communitarian vision of change. This is the approach adopted by Stewart and some of his colleagues (for instance, Clarke and Stewart 1988, Stewart 1989a and b, and Stewart and Stoker 1988). The legislative changes of the late 1980s are analysed in terms of the extent to which they encourage different forms of initiative at local level, or present obstacles to them. This approach allows for a reinterpretation of the notion of an enabling authority in ways which allow for an increased involvement by active citizens at local level and a public service orientation, that is one 'which recognizes that services have to meet the need of the user *and* public purpose, and that this requires public authorities to be close to the public as customer but also close to the public as citizen in determining public purpose' (Stewart 1992, p. 36).

In a sense, proponents of this approach take the promise of the new right literally and seek to develop it in ways which undermine the intentions of its authors. They stress the notion of community government, building on the potentially strategic role left to local government and emphasize that the powers of local government should be extended to meet new needs. 'Local government is', it is argued, 'about local authorities facilitating the meeting of the needs and problems of their communities in the most effective way. It is an expression of the *enabling* authority, not in the narrow sense of enabling other organizations to do the work of the local authority – that is in its own way another inward-looking approach that defines the local authority not by the communities it serves, but by the services for which it is responsible – but in the sense of enabling communities to define and meet their needs' (Clarke and Stewart 1991, p. 62).

This approach questions notions of local government which start from service provision and which have tended to dominate debate on left and right since 1945. Stewart points out that some of these questions were being raised within the local government community well before the government legislation was proposed (Stewart 1989a, p. 175). An emphasis on service provision implies both high levels of expenditure and pressures for uniform levels of service across the country and means that there is always pressure for spending and policy direction to be controlled – or at least heavily influenced – from the centre. Instead, Stewart and his colleagues argue for a much broader definition focused on the needs and problems of the communities concerned, arguing (like Holliday's new suburban right, but with rather different ambitions) for a move to community or local government, rather than local administration (Clarke and Stewart 1991, pp. 1–11). Stewart suggests that for this to work an enabling authority needs to have access to many different forms of intervention – direct provision would not be ruled out, but nor would it have a privileged position. He goes on to argue for a responsible and accountable authority which would 'provide services not to the public, but for the public and with the public' and require a more active involvement by its citizens in decision-making (Stewart 1989b, p. 241). The importance of distinguishing between citizens and consumers is stressed to reinforce the argument that local government cannot be reduced to a series of straightforward commercial or service delivery transactions. Instead, it is suggested, that it must both provide services and be concerned with the rights of its citizens – it must be concerned both with 'equity, justice and citizenship' and with 'responsiveness, quality and customer' (Clarke and Stewart 1991, p. 40).

The need for user involvement and to building responsiveness is emphasized and the message is not merely relevant to local government. Ranson and Stewart comment more generally on public sector management, that its dual task 'is to enable the reflective participation of citizens but also the government of collective action in the public interest' (Ranson and Stewart 1989, p. 19). But in the local government context it would also suggest an increased level of decentralization, and councils covering significantly smaller areas and representing much smaller populations, which sounds rather like the pre-1974 rural and urban district councils, and sits rather uneasily alongside the strategic élites identified by Brooke in his rather different consideration of the enabling authority. Crouch and Marquand also suggest that government organizations based on population units of three to eight million people may be the most appropriate for the development of effective policy-making between public authorities and business organizations (Crouch and Marquand 1989, p. xi).

Evidence for the feasibility of some of the proposals they make is drawn by Stewart and his colleagues from the recent experience of local government in Britain (see, for example, Stewart and Stoker 1988), and sometimes from the experience of local government in other European countries (such as Scandinavia, Stewart and Stoker 1989a, pp. 125–42; Stoker develops similar points in his introduction to a collection of articles on local government in Europe, Stoker 1991b, pp. 15–16). Within Britain the new possibilities identified include the growth of economic development activity at local level, which suggests that a broader interpretation of the local government role is required than that of service provider – the significance of economic development work has now also been given formal recognition in the Local Government and Housing Act (see, for example, Stoker 1989b, pp. 128–9). As Stewart notes, 'It is significant . . . that this new function has involved them in working in a wide variety of ways to assist other organizations and individuals rather than acting directly' (Stewart 1989b, p. 249).

Similar arguments are also developed by Hambleton and Hoggett in their analysis of decentralization strategies which have been undertaken by local governments of different political stripes. They suggest that there are two main possibilities for development in the 1990s – market pluralism and pluralist collectivism (Hambleton and Hoggett 1987, Hambleton et al. 1989, Hambleton 1990, Figure 2). The latter is very close to the enabling and participative model developed by Stewart and others, although it is focused more particularly on the implications of decentralization initiatives, the potential growth of not-for-profit organizations and trusts to meet public needs and the value of direct democracy (Hambleton 1990, pp. 114 and 126). The arguments in favour of developing such a model seem to have a wide resonance within local government (see also Gyford 1991, for example) and the Local Government Management Board, in particular, is taking them up and developing them in much of its training material (see, for example, LGTB 1987). In a report prepared for the Local Government Training Board on the relationship between local government and the voluntary sector, Gutch and Young argue that local authorities need 'to look more closely at their roles and their relationships with other local actors, not in a suspicious or competitive way, but in the spirit of shared commitment to local democracy, local control and partnership' (Gutch and Young 1988).

FAILING TO FIND IT

Stewart's analysis contains a powerful critique of the policies of the Thatcher governments, which he takes to task for limiting the scope for moving towards the world of community government and reducing opportunities for public accountability (Stewart 1989b). The most powerful element of these arguments is perhaps the alternative vision they contain. It is a remarkable – almost heroic – statement of what might be possible, in other circumstances, if the government were prepared to develop some elements of its programme while minimizing others (see particularly Stewart and Stoker 1988). In many ways it is a valuable antidote to the fatalism of the early 1980s. But as a picture of what has taken place (and in a sense what is likely to take place in the near future) it is ultimately unconvincing. Here, as in the previous chapter, it is difficult to distinguish between hopes, ambitions and visions and the analysis of change. It seems agreed that local government is being fragmented (or devolved) with the clear identification of direct service organizations, cost centres and the use of agencies outside local government for service delivery. It is less clear that an 'enabling authority' such as that favoured by Stewart is really on the horizon. Practitioners and politicians within local government are not in a position to deliver what he suggests and might not be prepared to if they were, unless they could be guaranteed greater influence and access to more resources. The future for elected local government looks rather more bleak.

It is perhaps rather more likely that the strategic managers will be able to develop 'enabling authorities' which suit them rather better and give them increased status. But the implied assumption (of Brooke, Holliday and Stewart) is that elected local governments are the most likely and most appropriate bodies to undertake the role of making order out of chaos, of taking on the co-ordinating and strategic role and of developing local political leadership. Unfortunately – as they all recognize – some aspects of the reforms of the 1980s make it more difficult to achieve this, whether because by stressing competitiveness they tend to undermine the value of local political initiative or simply because they restrict the powers and financial resources available at local level. While it may in principle be appropriate for local government to stress and seek to develop its strategic political (governmental) role, it is difficult to see what it has to offer to those it seeks to govern. It has lost (or is about to lose) many of its direct service responsibilities and has not yet gained any corresponding legal powers.

Here, of course, competitors are already beginning to put themselves forward – from various joint committees, to training and enterprise councils, health authorities and (looming on the horizon) regional levels of government. Even the police have begun to influence other agencies through community policing to the extent that they sometimes present their role as close to that of social work (see, for example, Brake and Hale 1992, ch. 4). Despite the formal position of local authorities as lead agency in the field of community care, for example, it is difficult not to see the increased emphasis of health authorities on primary health care, holistic approaches and health-led locality planning as encroaching on traditional local authority responsibilities (see, for example, Allen 1991). Since such moves reflect an understanding that the local social context may also lead to health problems, they also imply an increased intervention by health professionals outside the traditional confines of the hospital, surgery and health visiting. They imply that it is necessary to work with a range of agencies (which might, of course, include the local authority as well as a range of voluntary and community organizations) to achieve their principal ends through forms of co-ordination and networking. In other words, health authorities, too, have a claim (in some policy areas at least) to being the agencies which should be bringing order out of chaos.

In a sense the notion of an enabling authority relies on a local authority being in a relatively powerful position compared to other actors. There is a final twist in the tail of the new arrangements, even for the strategic managers who hope to see their role enhanced by them. Many of their hopes are based on the belief that they can effectively direct 'providers' through the issuing and monitoring of contracts. And in many cases they may be able to do so, although it is also (as was argued in Chapter 3) dangerous to exaggerate the potential effectiveness of contracts, particularly when they are drawn up with relatively powerful organizations. Where the 'provider' bodies are not commercial organizations, the situation is likely to be murkier still. In some cases it is already clear that some non-statutory agencies have their own independent power and can effectively dictate the terms on which they are prepared to co-operate with councils. Most councils which wish to develop social housing, for example, now have to rely on co-operation from major housing associations which have their own priorities and are in a strong negotiating rather than a contracting relationship (see, for example, Houlihan 1988). In other policy areas, the relationship is simply becoming more complicated and it is not easy to predict what the outcomes are likely to be. They may vary from place to place, with the form of service delivery being influenced by the priorities of the agency undertaking the task. National organizations such as the National Society for the Prevention of Cruelty to Children and the National Children's Home, both of which operate in conjunction with local authority social services departments in different places, have their own nationally agreed strategic aims and ways of operating, which are unlikely to be set aside simply because of some arrangement made at local level.

In other cases voluntary – community based – bodies may be largely dependent on local authority funding and find it difficult to challenge the councils which support them, without taking enormous financial risks. The relationship may involve the construction of tight forms of control which are perceived as excessively demanding rather than enabling, since voluntary organizations are highly dependent on their financial backers and may find themselves under far more extensive forms of inspection (see Hadley and Hatch 1981, pp. 157–9). As dependent – almost client – organizations they are likely to exercise a high degree of self-censorship, instead of surviving as independent and autonomous organizations working alongside local governments. Yet it could be argued that these are precisely the organizations which ought to be most independent and representative of their communities and least influenced by council priorities.

Problems of accountability are difficult to avoid with an enabling council, since it is increasingly unclear who is actually responsible for what particular service – its funding and delivery. This can be seen particularly clearly in the case of voluntary organizations since if a council's financial resources are constrained (as they are likely to be for the foreseeable future) then the easiest cuts to make are always likely to be those of organizations outside the council, particularly grants to organizations not delivering core services for it. This is also likely to make developing good relationships with voluntary agencies problematic simply because it is not possible to sustain funding levels consistently from year to year. Alexander raises a rather different concern, pointing to the increased need in an enabling authority to develop two forms of accountability. The first involves the specifying or contracting side of the councils work. Here the council is publicly accountable to the electorate. But different forms of accountability are involved in the complex set of 'contractual and quasi-commercial relationships between the council, acting on behalf of the community, and other agencies whose links to the community are limited to the point at which they deliver services to it' (Alexander 1991, p. 73). This second form of accountability (a consequence of the enabling aspect of the council's work) will tend to be 'non-democratic and technical' with the danger that 'in a network composed of a series of bilateral contractual relationships it will come to dominate' (ibid., p. 74). 'There is a danger', continues Alexander, 'that the argument in favour of democracy and accountability will be lost by default as the energy of managers is directed exclusively to the technical issues raised by fragmentation and politicians continue to behave as if nothing, or nothing much, has changed' (ibid., p. 76).

It is tempting, though perhaps unfair, to look back at some of the managerial and academic enthusiasm which greeted the first wave of corporate planning literature in the late 1960s and early 1980s, as attempts were made to transfer ideas from the private sector directly into the local government system, and to remember how modest the changes actually were in the end. Much of the writing on the enabling authority is still about what might be, rather than what is, and even reports back on particular cases read rather too much like the similar reports of success we heard with such regularity from other (and sometimes the same) places in the early 1970s (expressed, for example, in the papers collected and analysed by Greenwood and Stewart 1974).

The discussion of the enabling authority is helpful in highlighting the extent to which each local authority is increasingly one agency among many at local level. Insofar as the intention is to emphasize the potential fragility of local government's status within that more 'pluralist' environment then it is a useful notion. It emphasizes the need for those working in and elected to positions within local government to work for the right to be seen as representative of their communities and to be the agencies around which others should cluster. In that sense it does give the strategic managers a role, if they can take it; just as it gives the local politicians a role if they can win it. The important point, however, is that such a role cannot be taken for granted: it may be that 'chaos' is simply accepted or that some other agency or agencies take on the lead role. It is not clear that the most likely urban or local regimes in the 1990s will be organized around elected local government. The next two chapters consider some of the new arrangements at local level which limit the possibilities for moves towards any kind of enabling authority, although it remains likely that the strategic managers and leading politicians will retain a position within local policy élites.

Chapter Five

Post-Fordism and local government

One of the weaknesses of the approaches discussed in the last few chapters is that they tend to discuss changes within local government as if they were the product of more or less rational political debate within identifiable policy communities. This means that they tend to play down, minimize or ignore the wider context within which the moves are taking place. Yet it is increasingly clear that approaching the analysis of change within the local government system as if it were independent of wider social and economic shifts is fundamentally misleading. At the very least, changing economic and social structures may restrict or open up opportunities. And they may also be providing the foundations for more extensive adjustments. Setting change in the wider context of post-war restructuring should allow us to raise our heads above the parapet of local government, to identify potentially more significant shifts in the operation of local and national politics.

As we have seen there is widespread agreement that the position of local government within the British state system has changed significantly over the last 25 years but rather less agreement about how the new arrangements should be characterized. Similar difficulties arise with the attempts which have been made to analyse the nature of wider changes in economy, society and politics over the same period. One set of arguments has clustered around moves towards fragmentation and flexibility in the labour process and away from models based on mass production and mass consumption of relatively standardized products and away from Keynesian welfare states. Stress has been placed on geographical specialization and a growth in interaction between localities and regions within an increasingly global system.

Some of these arguments have been set within theoretical frameworks which suggest a move from modernism to post-modernism (see, for example, Lash and Urry 1987), whilst others have stressed the importance of 'flexible specialization' while explicitly avoiding the use of wider systemic labels (see, for example, Hirst 1989). This chapter, however, will focus on approaches which use the terms Fordism and post-Fordism (or neo-Fordism) as the axes around which to construct their arguments[1]. The main reason for such a focus is that it seems to be the most developed of the positions with respect to local government in Britain, and many of the points made within that framework can also be directed to the other positions. Another reason for doing so is simply that the terms have almost entered the common sense of the contemporary social sciences in ways which cut across customary disciplinary, theoretical and political allegiances. It is as if we all know that something important is going on and feel better if it can be labelled (see, for example, Coates' discussion of British politics since 1945, Coates 1991).

POST-FORDISM AS TECHNOLOGICAL PARADIGM

In different ways, Geddes, Hoggett, Murray and Stoker have all drawn on theories of post-Fordism, in their analyses of changes in the local government sphere. Hoggett was one of the first explicitly to pull the discussion of local government into debates about state restructuring and the crisis of Fordism. He showed the need to move beyond the confines of traditional local government studies and to develop a broader framework with the help of which it might be possible to understand what was happening. His work has been taken up and used by others in developing their arguments about notions of local government in the post Fordist period (for example, it is acknowledged as a crucial base by Geddes 1988 and, rather more cautiously, by Stoker 1989a). Hoggett's early contribution is significant, therefore, not only in its own right, but also as a crucial marker on which others have been able to build and generalize.

Although he also refers to the arguments of Aglietta, Hoggett (1987) draws largely on what Elam (1990) describes as a neo-Schumpeterian perspective on the debates about Fordism and post-Fordism. This explains the history of capitalism as a history of technological revolutions, following a pattern of long waves of economic development. He builds substantially on approaches which identify a succession of technological or techno-economic paradigms (reflected in, for example, Freeman 1987, Freeman and Perez 1988, and Perez 1986) in which the driving force of wider social and economic change is a series of key – technological – factors. Within this model, post-Fordism is associated with the rise of a new paradigm organized around the rise of information technology and the use of microelectronics, which implies the development of a new set of socio-institutional relationships. According to Freeman, Fordism was largely characterized by assembly line mass production, whereas post-Fordism means the rise of flexible manufacturing and networking between agencies, with the help of information technology (Freeman 1987, Table 15). The new 'technological style' based around the extensive introduction of information technology is said to encourage (possibly require) the spread of more decentralized production methods, breaking 'down the separation of "head" and "hands" that was the hallmark of Fordism. Hence job enlargement, the delegation of inspection and quality control to workers, group technology, participative shop floor practices and so on can be seen as harbingers of a new techno-managerial paradigm' (Hoggett 1987, p. 221).

Hoggett's argument proceeds by a process of analogy from a broad statement of what has happened and can be (more or less) noted in the production sphere to what has happened or is happening in the welfare state and local government within that. The analogy is based on the notion that 'professionals' operate as 'people processors' in the 'assembly line' through which the Keynesian welfare state produces and delivers its services. Hoggett argues that, like production in the private sector, production in the Keynesian welfare state has been inflexibly geared towards the output of a few standardized products with economies of scale constantly emphasized. He suggests that the system resembled Fordism without Ford – a kind of mongrel paradigm based on an uneasy marriage between a pre-Fordist craft (professional) productive system and a Taylorized (rational-bureaucratic) system' (ibid., p. 223).

Local government, able to resist the logic of the previous technological revolution, is, according to this argument, ripe for the shifts promised by the present one. Within this model the old sites for resistance become the seedbeds in which the new technological revolution will flourish, although Hoggett acknowledges a continued bureaucratic 'conservatism' in some areas which may require 'left' politicians to drag local government managers into the second half of the twentieth century. He predicts the development of 'new organizational and managerial forms strikingly reminiscent of the newer "hi-tech" companies of the M4 corridor: leaner and flatter managerial structures, decentralized "cost and innovation centres" (i.e. district or neighbourhood offices with their own devolved budgets, powers over recruitment, performance indicators, etc.), enlarged and more generic roles, team working, flexibility and infor- mality, responsive back-line support to the front-line staff and so on' (ibid., p. 225).

There are a number of problems with this version of the post-Fordist model, particularly as it applies to local government and the local state. One is simply the implied determinism: it appears that these changes are bound to take place although local governments are offered some choice in how they may be taken up. This also seems to be the gist of Geddes' argument, since his critique of the GLC suggests that its officers and politicians did not take full advantage of the scope for beginning to revolutionize 'the social relations of the state' (Geddes 1988, p. 112). Despite some attempts at modifying the strength of their arguments, allowing more independent scope for change in 'socio-institutional' frameworks, for Freeman and Perez 'the history of capitalism remains one where "new" techno-economic forces always do the initial acting and "old" socio-institutional frameworks the eventual reacting' (Elam 1990, p. 12). In his more recent writing, Hoggett has substantially shifted the emphasis of his argument, stressing that 'the modernization processes at work today have no inexorable logic to them, that they are similarly compatible with a range of social choices' (Hoggett 1990, p. 2). He outlines a series of qualifications before going on to identify post-Fordism as 'the "deep structure" of the coming period' (ibid., p. 5) or the 'new logic of capitalist development' (ibid., p. 15) which determines the range of available choices or 'a new basic template or paradigm' which allows for a range of basic types (Hoggett 1991, p. 243). However qualified the argument, political processes still tend to be relegated to secondary status. This makes it difficult to explain why particular technological opportuni- ties are taken up at one time rather than another, and also makes it easy to under-estimate the extent to which the direction of change remains contested.

The second major weakness of Hoggett's argument is the way in which it draws an analogy between the spheres of production and the local welfare state. Superficially the analogy is quite attractive, but there is a real danger of exaggerating the significance of a metaphor of this sort which does not hold up very well under sustained scrutiny. Hoggett's acknowledgement of a 'mongrel paradigm' itself undermines it. A key point about 'street-level bureaucrats' – to borrow Lipsky's eloquent phrase – such as teachers and social workers, is precisely that they are expected to make decisions based on individual discretion where bureau-cratic rules do not apply very well. They are trapped between their 'clients' and their 'employers', with only their 'professionalism' to pull them through. The detailed differences and discretion make it difficult to process people *en masse*, according to rational-bureaucratic rules. Instead of pointing up a similarity, in effect Hoggett's arguments are most successful in indicating a sharp set of differences between the two spheres. Yet clearly the welfare state professionals are products of Fordism by any definition of the term, since without the (Fordist) welfare state they could not exist. This makes the attempt to identify pre-Fordist 'craft' elements in their work unconvincing, even if it is clear that their labour process is not (yet?) Taylorist.

POST-FORDISM AND REGULATION THEORY

Not all of these criticisms of Hoggett's approach (which apply with particular force to his early paper) can be applied to all those using the terms Fordism and post-Fordism. There are many Fordisms and, consequently, also many post-Fordisms. Lipietz, for example, who would be highly critical of any generalizing theory of this type, explicitly distances himself from long wave and systemic analysis and comments that 'the emergence of a new regime of accumulation is not a pre-ordained part of capitalism's destiny, even though it may correspond to certain identifiable "tendencies"' (Lipietz 1987, p. 15). There is a fundamental difference of emphasis between those who focus largely on the production process (as Hoggett does) and those who are more concerned to focus on the interaction between regimes of accumulation and modes of regulation (such as Lipietz and others within the regulation school; see also Painter 1991b). Even while each is apparently discussing the same phenomena, and using what looks like the same terminology, they have quite different theoretical starting points. Lipietz stresses that 'regimes of accumulation and modes of regulation are chance discoveries made in the course of human struggles and if they are for a while successful, it is only because they are able to ensure a certain regularity and a certain permanence in social reproduction' (Lipietz 1987, p. 15). Lipietz is by no means clear that a neo- (or post-) Fordism is currently being constructed. Certainly it is an open question rather than a necessary process. Nor is he convinced of the form such resolution to the crisis of Fordism will take. One option may even be a more centralized and automated form of Taylorism (Amin 1989, p. 14).

Jessop neatly summarizes the underlying argument of the regulationists as follows: 'They asked how capitalism could survive even though the capital relation itself inevitably generated antagonisms and crises which made continuing accumulation improbable. They found an answer in specific institutional forms, societal norms, and patterns of strategic conduct which both expressed and regulated these conflicts until the inevitable tensions and divergencies among these various regulatory forms reached crisis point' (Jessop 1988, p. 149). And, as Aglietta argues, 'the resolution of a crisis always involves an irreversible transformation of the mode of production' and capitalism 'can escape from its contemporary organic crisis only by generating a new cohesion, a neo-Fordism' (Aglietta, 1979, pp. 19 and 385). So, if the crisis is being resolved in some way, then it can only be on the basis of a move towards such a new cohesion. The identification of post-Fordism by writers such as Murray (1989) is predicated on the belief that such a move is underway, and a set of characteristics of both periods (stressing a move from mass production to increased flexibility) identified to confirm that this is the case (see also Harvey 1989a, ch. 9, who favours the term flexible accumulation to characterize the new period).

Stoker sets out to explore recent changes in local government within the broad framework of regulation theory. His arguments are carefully qualified, pointing to the possibility of counter tendencies developing, and stressing that he 'does not see the reform programme as rising automatically from the processes of social and economic change. Rather . . . it is part of the Thatcher Government's response to these processes. The aim is to create a local government compatible with the flexible economic structures, two-tier welfare system and enterprise culture which in the Thatcher vision constitute the key to a successful future' (Stoker 1989a, p. 159). Although he refers to Hoggett and Geddes, the conclusions he draws from them are modest. He returns to many of the familiar examples of change, in particular marketization, contracting out, and a new emphasis on consumers. But he approaches them from a rather different angle, stressing the extent to which they may parallel shifts in the private sector, going so far as to suggest that with information technology it is not too difficult to see local government as a sort of public sector Benetton, through which information may pass out to a set of service providing contractors (ibid., p. 166). His stress is on the development of a dual welfare system within which the weak (and the poor) will have to rely on increasingly minimal local welfare while the better off may gain access to private (or better public) welfare, by topping up with their own resources. He is less concerned than others to identify possible strategies of resistance (although he does refer to the possible development of a wider public service orientation and community government, which, of course he discusses more fully elsewhere). His post-Fordism is a rather more bleak (and overall more convincing) vision than that of Hoggett.

But some of the weaknesses of the model developed by Hoggett are also apparent in Stoker's arguments. Most important, the nature of Fordist local government remains elusive. It is in this context that Hoggett's arguments are introduced, and even as qualified by Stoker, they do not quite fit. The allegedly Fordist model stressing functionalism, uniformity and hierarchy listed by Stoker (1989a, p. 151, and borrowed from Stewart) may be an accurate enough reflection of the formal structures of local government, building as they do on the legislative framework bequeathed from the nineteenth century or expressed in the ideal types of Weber (see, for example, Pollitt 1986, p. 159), but they bear little relationship to what actually happened in Britain after 1945. Elsewhere Stewart has acknowledged both the lack of uniformity and the importance of internal bargaining within authorities, noting the importance of competing professional ideologies (Stewart 1983, p. 102) and, of course, many of the detailed decisions of those allocating resources in housing departments, social services departments, and 'delivering services' in schools have involved significant variation. Stoker, too, in another context himself seems to accept a rather more complicated picture of organizational politics within local authorities (Stoker and Wilson 1986).

One consequence of the new arrangements may, in any case, be an increase in formal hierarchy, determined by detailed contracts in some areas, leaving still less scope for practical initiative at the level of delivery. It is not clear why private sector organizations contracted to undertake specific tasks should have any incentive to vary their activity in response to expressed need without negotiating a new contract. This may be the price which has to be paid for the loss of the 'public service orientation'. As argued in the last chapter some forms of contracting may encourage the development of close sets of relationships between favoured suppliers and particular local governments in ways which obscure processes of decision-making and reduce the prospects of 'control' from above. The process of contracting out on the one hand encourages openness and competitiveness – since it is competitive tendering – but it also encourages a closure, since decisions have to be made and bids considered which may involve matters of commercial confidence. It is difficult to open such matters to public debate, which leaves them in the hands of the senior managers and élite politicians, effectively reinforcing the powers of those at the top of the hierarchy (or in network terms, at the centre of the spider's web). Government proposals explicitly to separate the roles of councillors responsible for the purchaser/contractor sides of local government and those responsible for the continuing provider/service delivery sides (who might formally be contracted to undertake specific tasks through an internal market) would merely reinforce this division if implemented.

The use of contracts may also effectively reduce rather than increase flexibility since, as Stewart argues, it is likely to reduce the scope for flexibility by fixing arrangements for relatively long periods and making renegotiation difficult (for example by involving fee renegotiations) (Stewart 1989a). It is unclear who will have the effective power in the new arrangements on the issuing of contracts. Here the comparison with Benetton, Marks and Spencer and Next (developed by Murray 1987) may be useful since they clearly have power over their suppliers, who are dependent on them for large orders. It is not so clear that that will be the case for local governments, competing between themselves, and possibly having to negotiate with monopoly (or near monopoly) suppliers. Such negotiations may even encourage more rather than less standardization.

The experience of the GLC's economic policies, on which Murray draws to argue for the opportunities offered by flexible specialization, may suggest that it is possible to intervene effectively in those areas where the authority is dominant, but they also show how difficult it is to be effective in areas where other agencies are dominant (Murray 1987; see also Mackintosh and Wainwright 1987). In practice the GLC (and its investment arm GLEB) was not able to have the impact it hoped for. Its interventions into the private sector were generally small scale and usually in sectors or firms in decline. GLEB had little scope to develop its complex system of planning agreements and in the end their executives were more concerned with introducing (Fordist?) methods of commercial management into relatively backward firms struggling for survival than with restructuring sectors of the economy – whatever the initial ambitions to 'restructure for labour' may have been. As Mackintosh and

Wainwright conclude from the London experience: 'a local authority, however large, has precious little leverage. Investment decisions in the private sector, which sustain or destroy employment, are made by large, often multinational, firms with an eye to their balance sheets' (Mackintosh and Wainwright 1987, p. 13).

The value of the Fordist/post-Fordist distinction is perhaps more apparent if the focus remains on the role of the Keynesian welfare state as part of Fordism as a mode of regulation. As a crucial component of that state it is easy to see how the crisis of Fordism would also undermine the local welfare state. But, clearly even within Fordism, the model of local welfare varied significantly between countries – above all, some of the features identified by Stoker as elements of post-Fordism in the future for Britain are precisely those which have tended to dominate in the USA throughout the Fordist epoch. Not only is there a dramatically greater variety in forms of local government in the USA, to the extent that Hambleton comments that 'even within one state there may be more diversity than within the whole of the UK' (Hambleton 1990, p. 24), but also some of the better known forms fit well with a post-Fordist scenario – including strong-mayor models, the appointment of council managers and commission structures (ibid., pp. 24–5). Smith describes the US welfare state as one based on the contracting out of state responsibilities to private actors. He concludes that, 'In this form of state structure "the state" is difficult for the average citizen to grasp as a "public" entity. Because state intervention takes place by indirect policies which induce parts of civil society to act, rather than by direct action by public administrators, it is very difficult for popular political forces to hold "the state" accountable for its extensive enmeshment in everyday economic and social life' (Smith 1988, p. 40).

PROBLEMS WITH FORDISM

But, more important questions remain to be settled. One which underlies the whole discussion, is whether the Fordism/post-Fordism distinction is broadly a useful one and it is perhaps worth noting (as Stoker himself also does, Stoker 1990) that some, at least, of the post-Fordist theories have recently been under serious challenge on their home territories. Drawing on these more critical debates Meegan substantially questions the notion of Fordism which is necessary before any move towards post-Fordism is possible. In other words he questions Hoggett's confidence (and indeed that of many other contributors to the debate) that Fordism is an unproblematic concept. In particular he argues that neither manufacturing industry, nor the mass production industries within it ever played the dominant part which theories of Fordism suggest they did. In the context of Britain, for example, he points to the importance of the service sector over a long period, as well as the significance of industrial sectors (such as mechanical engineering, which accounted for 12.8 per cent of manufacturing employment in 1968) in which small batch production dominated and to others (such as the chemical industry which accounted for 8.7 per cent at the same time) in which automated flow production dominated (Meegan 1988 pp. 152–63). The search for post-Fordist forms of flexible specialization in the modern economy has also aroused controversy, with writers such as Williams et al. (1987) arguing that the extent of change has been much exaggerated and Sayer suggesting that the successful growth of Japanese industry seems to owe a great deal to what look rather more like Fordist arrangements. Sayer makes the point that:

> 'the trouble with concepts like Fordism, post-Fordism and flexible specialization is that they are overly flexible and insufficiently specialized'. [He goes on to argue that] 'the literature on post-Fordism is confused in its arguments, long on speculation and hype, and based on selected examples whose limited sectoral, spatial and temporal range is rarely acknowledged'
>
> *(Sayer 1989, p. 666)*

He sharply criticizes both the dominant models of Fordism and its supposed successor, suggesting that comparative studies of different economies may 'serve us better than binary histories' (Sayer, 1989, p. 691).

Whether or not these criticisms are finally to be fatal for the theories they should certainly make one rather more careful about using them uncritically. It makes it difficult to agree with Hoggett's comment that 'one of the few advantages of the term "post-Fordism" is its agnosticism about the future, i.e. it suggests that we're clearer about where we're coming from than where we're going to' (Hoggett 1991, p. 243). One of the central problems with arguments which start from the identification of a wider move from Fordism to post-Fordism is that it is possible to acknowledge the existence of many of the changes which have been identified, without yet being convinced that they have taken place as part of that shift. Rustin argues strongly that there is no reason to expect a clear relationship between the end of mass production and the rise of 'flexible consumer-driven systems of welfare' (Rustin 1989, p. 59). He sees post-Fordism as a model or strategy under contention, rather than 'a valid totalizing description of an emerging social formation here and now' (ibid., p. 61). He stresses the importance of political choice. The cost of acknowledging that a wider structural shift is taking place and locating local government within it, is that the whole process becomes a 'necessary' one, however that 'necessity' is qualified. There is a danger that every piece of evidence for fragmentation and decentralization, and every claim for flexibility is accepted at face value because it fits into the model, when it should be interrogated more fully. Once these questions begin to be asked, it is less clear why theories such as those associated with post-Fordism are needed at all. In particular, it is unclear why each capitalist crisis and its resolution has to be explained in terms of a major system shift or structural change as Aglietta suggests.

Regulation theory is such a protean beast, however, that in some versions at least these criticisms may find little purchase. Some argue that its strength is precisely that it is so open-ended – Elam, for example, emphasizes that the approach encourages an 'enhanced interest in the peculiarities of historical/cultural contexts and greater attention to "ethnographic detail"' (Elam 1990, p. 33) and stresses the point that for its French originators, even if Fordism can be identified, the form of its replacement remains open. Jessop et al. go further to suggest that Britain was never fully Fordist and, therefore, unlikely to become fully post-Fordist (Jessop et al. 1989, p. 99). They identify features which look more like pre- and post-Fordism in the post-war period, and point to some elements of Fordism likely to survive and even expand into the 1990s. Unlike Stoker, they argue that Thatcher was obstructing rather than assisting with Britain's shift to post-Fordism (p. 83). As the qualifications accumulate the problem then becomes one of determining what the theory has to offer that is fundamentally distinctive. Perhaps it can be summarized as a Marxism which is not determinist and calls for sensitivity to the importance of social and political institutions as part of the social organization of production. Such a development is very much to be welcomed, but it is not clear that producing what looks like a new generalizing model really delivers the goods.

If, however, the model is reduced – as it frequently seems to be – to an ideal type, then it loses its force, becoming little more than a typology with little to say about the dynamics of change (see, for example, Stoker 1990). A list can be made of the features of the past and the present and they can be labelled Fordist and post-Fordist (see, for example, Rustin 1989, pp. 56–7). That may be satisfying – like cataloguing butterflies – but it means that some of the answers which the approach appeared to deliver have been lost. The strength of the regulation approach is that it predicts that a system change must be taking place and it suggests some of the lines which such a change is likely to follow (even if those lines are becoming increasingly difficult to follow as the theory is modified). Of course, this is also its weakness since it is always in danger of slipping into determinism. Unfortunately moving as far away from the model as Stoker does leaves his analysis without the (Marxist) driving force which underlies it so that it is little more than a checklist whose elements still need to be justified.

It sometimes look as if the theorists of post-Fordist local government (Hoggett as well as Stoker) want to have it both ways: on the one hand the theoretical approach implies a structural shift, whose key features can be identified from first principles; but as soon as its proponents are accused of determinism, or it is suggested that some of the changes it appears to predict are not taking place, then the notion of post-Fordism becomes increasingly slippery and, as Sayer suggests, almost as flexible as the specialization which it claims to identify. It is nevertheless important to acknowledge that these debates have drawn attention to significant changes which are taking place, and have taken the important first steps of relating local government to those changes. At the risk of being accused of heresy, it is possible to draw on some of the key insights of authors such as Jessop and Harvey, as well as Hoggett and Stoker, who have associated themselves with the Fordist/post-Fordist distinction, without having to take on that model. This is done more explicitly in the next chapter.

It is necessary to position local government within the wider post-war settlement – a vital part of the Keynesian welfare state – as the theorists of post-Fordism do, because it confirms that it is not a free floating institution but part of the wider British polity, set within the framework of a changing political economy. It is also important to locate it within a wider set of changing international or global relations which may be changing the context for local politics. But it is important not to underestimate the importance of the welfare state and the local state within it as part of a political settlement. If, however, it is viewed as a continually contested element, within a basically political compromise then the consequences of its break up are likely to be rather different, and rather more fluid, too. Leys describes the compromise as constituting a 'new political order, incorporating the labour movement, [and leading to] . . . a general acceptance of many of the tenets of social democracy: that capitalism could and should be made acceptable to "ordinary people" by being regulated, humanized, and made to support a comprehensive system of social security' (Leys 1989, p. 63). The settlement itself always looked rather less stable than anything labelled 'Fordism' might be expected to be – in Britain, 'it was a political contract built on an unsustainable economic basis, requiring the pursuit of impossible economic objectives, an instability constitutive of the post-war settlement itself' (Schwarz 1987, p. 115).

NOTE

1 Some authors, including Hoggett, Aglietta and Lipietz, use the term neo-Fordism in preference to post-Fordism. Lipietz and Aglietta refer to a potential neo-Fordism to indicate that the crisis of Fordism is not yet resolved. In this paper the term post-Fordism is used deliberately because most of the arguments under discussion (including those of Hoggett) seem to proceed from an assumption that a fundamentally new set of arrangements is being introduced.

Chapter Six

Restructuring the local welfare state

The stress of the dominant approaches to the analysis of local government in the 1980s and 1990s is placed on flexibility or fragmentation, with local government becoming one (perhaps the first) among many providers or becoming the regulator of a wider range of provision offered by others. In a sense such approaches simply take for granted the existing formal structures of local governance (as elected local government organized through councils) and seek to find a place for those councils in the new world of the 1990s. If a broader approach is taken (i.e. one which is concerned with the local welfare state rather than a narrowly defined local government or local administration) then the picture may begin to change and it becomes possible to develop a more complex understanding of urban or local politics. It also becomes possible to locate the other analyses within a broader framework, without being under constant pressure to 'defend' local government.

This chapter will argue that the restructuring of the local welfare state in Britain since the mid-1970s has taken place along two main axes: the first of these has involved a redefinition of welfare and the second the development of different forms of political representation. In the wider context of Western capitalist states, Bob Jessop has summarized this process, possibly a little inelegantly but nevertheless very helpfully, as a shift from Keynesian welfare state to Schumpeterian workfare state (Jessop 1992; see also Jessop 1991, pp. 95–104, although he does not use these terms there). In the former 'welfare' is defined as a right to certain minimum standards: in the latter welfare is defined in terms of economic success – on the competitive success of enterprise (elsewhere I have used the term enterprise state to make a similar point about the shift which has taken place, Cochrane 1991, pp. 290–2). Jessop defines the distinctive aims of the Schumpeterian workfare state as being 'to promote product, process organizational and market innovation in open economies in order to strengthen as far as possible the structural competitiveness of the national economy' and 'to subordinate social policy to the needs of labour market flexibility and/or to the constraints of international competition' (Jessop 1992, p. 1). This implies a significant change at local level, since it is competition between places intra- and internationally which provides the driving force for the new arrangements rather than the delivery of a centrally agreed package of more or less universal services (see, for example, Cooke 1990, Cox and Mair 1991 and Harvey 1989a).

WELFARE AS COMPETITION

This broader shift in the nature of the local welfare state is not only identified by critics, but has also been put forward more positively as a necessary strategy by its supporters. Bennett and Krebs, for example, set this out very clearly, emphasizing the view that economic growth in local areas 'can follow only from the development of a new capacity to respond to global economic change' (Bennett and Krebs 1991, p. 6). They build on this to argue that local government needs to be more business-like, literally more like a business, and not only in the field of economic development. They want to see a change in focus – what they call a move beyond welfare – in which local well-being becomes defined as economic success, based on close liaison (or partnership) between council and business: 'to work it requires the whole of the council's approach to be planned to achieve the required economic objectives and to balance these with wider service demands' (ibid., p. 177). The underlying assumptions of the local welfare state are to be turned on their head, but this revolutionary change is to be achieved not with the bang of legislation in Parliament but through the whimper of partnership at local level.

In this model, the orientation of welfare policy is increasingly and explicitly defined in terms which emphasize competition between places. One implication of this may be – as the Major Government argued in the context of negotiations with other EC governments over the Social Chapter of the Maastricht Treaty on European Union – that it is necessary to keep the costs of welfare down. But another possibility is that welfare provision itself may be defined in terms of its value to business rather than in terms of the needs of those dependent on welfare. At the risk of stating the obvious, the intention here is not to suggest that within the old structures of the Keynesian welfare state the needs of 'clients' or 'welfare dependents' were paramount. But it is important to highlight an important difference in emphasis, as a result of which the arguments of Marxists and neo-Marxists (such as Gough 1979) that the Keynesian welfare state basically operated in the interests of the reproduction of capitalism (even if it could not always deliver what it promised) have become the unacknowledged orthodoxy of the 1990s, so that it has become legitimate – indeed expected – for governments and business organizations to argue that this *should* be the case, even if they are less convinced that it already is.

It is also important to stress the extent to which the competition is localized – i.e. between places, not only between countries. This is a paradoxical consequence of the extent to which the economy has become globalized, so that in making their investment decisions major firms are able to compare and choose between individual locations, rather than countries (see, for example, Cooke 1989b, Robins 1990). They are able to take advantage of and build on the finer grained outcomes of the processes of uneven development – the spatial divisions of labour – identified by Doreen Massey (1984) and which themselves help to make different places what they are. One aspect of the localized competition is, perhaps, relatively obvious, expressed as it is in the mushroom growth of locally-based promotional and economic development activities which took place through the 1980s (see, for example, Campbell 1990 among many others). At local level, too, it has found expression in the increased emphasis on public–private partnership, linking business and government together in development schemes and in civic boosterism. The importance of differentiation in the competitive battle for employment, is widely accepted, and goes far beyond a narrow focus on economic development, fitting in with wider ambitions to strategic decision-making and image creation. A leading US management 'guru' sums this up in the argument that the 'idea of "what's special" about [a place] is decisive in determining the city's future' (Peters 1988, p. 143). The identification of special features has been a major feature of advertising campaigns in the late 1980s – picking up on the highly influential 'Glasgow's miles better' campaign. These have universally stressed the 'greenness' of the places being promoted, their receptiveness to high-tech and service employers, and where possible, their access to water-based sports facilities, which seems now to have become a measure of high status. Cultural differentiation, too, has become an increasing measure of activism, with Glasgow scooping the pool by winning designation as European City of Culture in 1990, but with Birmingham (attracting the Royal Ballet from Sadlers Wells) and Liverpool (with the Tate Gallery of the North) also heavily in contention. Even the corporate logos of many local authorities have been drawn into the battle. Only the more conservative (often Labour-controlled inner London boroughs) have been stuck with the modernist corporate symbolism of the early 1970s – the rest have moved on to historical skylines, or symbols which suggest that even the most industrial of cities nestles gently in the midst of rolling countryside, or at the heart of a scenic valley.

But a second aspect of the growing competition between places may be less obvious. An emphasis on competitiveness also implies the need for significant changes in those aspects of local government most closely associated with the welfare state. It may also be appropriate to develop different welfare strategies and welfare regimes in different places to fit with different local social formations (and particularly their economic and industrial structures). Some traditional welfare concerns (for example urban deprivation) may simply be reinterpreted as problems of economic growth, so that urban regeneration is redefined as business confidence and new construction (expressed for example in the setting up of urban development corporations). A stress on 'development' rather than welfare becomes dominant, but with the more or less explicitly stated assumption that urban regeneration through development will also improve matters for those who might otherwise have been recipients of welfare (see, for example, Harding's discussion of public–private partnerships, Harding 1990; see also Lewis 1992).

In extreme cases the whole issue is turned on its head, so that welfare provision is justified largely because of the way it make places more or less attractive to business: in one discussion of the need to develop policies to ensure that London retains its status as 'world city', for example, concern is expressed about the extent of urban deprivation experienced by the Bangladeshi community of Spitalfields, not because of the problems they face, but because it might reduce the quality of life for higher status residents and encourage businesses to relocate (Kennedy 1991, pp. 73–4).

Similarly the discussion of the need for affordable housing has less to do with those who can be expected to live in it and more to do with the needs of employers, since 'the market's inability to provide housing for lower-income households should be recognized as an impediment to London's development prospects' (ibid., p. 209).

Even where attempts are made to incorporate social regeneration more centrally into programmes of change the emphasis shifts because it is integrated into a business oriented vision. Sheffield's strategy for the year 2000 ('Sheffield 2000') was prepared through the Sheffield Economic Regeneration Committee (itself often put forward as a model of public–private partnership, see, for example, Fogarty and Christie 1990) and includes a well developed commitment to social regeneration (SERC, undated). In a sense, however, this positive expression helps to illustrate the extent of the changes and the ways in which they have influenced interpretations of 'welfare' as well as interpretations of 'enterprise' and economic regeneration. Sheffield's strategy is organized around a 'Vision' and has five main themes which come together to provide objectives, described as the 'Vision Becomes Reality objectives' because when they have been achieved the 'Vision' will indeed have become reality. Sheffield is to become: a natural centre for business and industry; a new decision centre; an international centre for sport, leisure and tourism; an international centre for teaching, learning, research and technology; and 'a city of life'.

It will be clear simply from reading the overall titles given to these themes that the first two are explicitly oriented towards business: the first affirms the desire to sustain and expand existing manufacturing, commercial and service industries and to attract new employers; the second builds on this to make claims to a share of office development and particularly the headquarters of national and international businesses. The second two in practice have a similar orientation since aiming to become an international centre for leisure and sport reflects ambitions to change the image of Sheffield (and the quality of life it has to offer) as much as any ambition to improve locally provided services. The stress on teaching, research and technology also reflects the selling of the city as one in which innovation and enterprise will flourish. In other words, the city's leisure and educational policies are seen as part of the selling of the city and an essential element of business infrastructure rather than being seen as a something provided for residents (the idea of providing anything *for* anybody is by now, of course, in any case almost universally derided within the new orthodoxy as a symbol of Fordist paternalism to be avoided at all costs). The final theme is more explicitly aimed towards social regeneration, aiming to create 'a positive environment for the health, benefit and enjoyment of all Sheffield people'. But even this positive expression is prefaced by the desire to 'foster a vibrant and dynamic city' (SERC, undated, p. 21) which implies a continued concern with image which owes more to business than to the needs of residents. Where the argument about social regeneration is developed further again stress is placed on the need to link economic regeneration and social regeneration, with the implication that the latter is dependent on the former, even if the obstacles which make it difficult for one to lead to the other still need to be overcome.

THE RISE OF PARTNERSHIP

There has been a marked blurring of the distinction between the public and the private, in terms of policy responsibility as much as in the form of service provision. In retrospect. Dearlove seems remarkably prescient in his analysis of the reorganization of local government which took place in the 1970s (even if his conclusions may have been a little premature) in identifying a concern about the lack of a formal relationship between 'economic power, social status and the political control of local government', and the extent to which political power was 'almost totally divorced from economic power' (Dearlove 1979, pp. 104–5). It is not difficult to see the period since the late 1970s as one in which those links have increasingly been forged more effectively. There has been a significant growth in business involvement – not just as supplier or market, or even as a model for management in local government, but as an active participant in the political process at local level. An early and rather modest expression of this can be seen in the requirement of local authorities to consult local businesses over rate levels and urban aid applications in the early 1980s, but the process has moved on apace since then (Grant 1987, p. 163).

The extent and significance of change is difficult to exaggerate. For most of the period since 1945 business in Britain has been markedly reluctant to become involved with local government. Few major companies are strictly locally based. Chambers of commerce have been notoriously weak compared to their counterparts in continental Europe, and have traditionally had little to say about most local government matters, except that planning rules are too tight, rates too high and that some sponsorship of overseas promotional trips may be helpful (see, for example, Stewart, M. 1984). The increased involvement of business in the processes of local government has been carefully constructed over the past decade, with help from central government, elected local governments and initiatives from the private sector. Central government has increasingly encouraged business leaders to take positions within more 'civic' arenas. It has done so in a number of ways. In some cases, it has simply set up local organizations whose structures involve business 'leaders' of one sort or another, and often appoints others whose main experience has been in the private, rather than the public sectors.

Perhaps the urban development corporations set up with specific powers over planning, the purchase and development of land in identified inner cities and with boards appointed from above have been the clearest recent example of this, but they have drawn on a relatively small part of the private sector, particularly that concerned with property development (Lewis 1992). In education, business is now expected to make a far more extensive contribution to the development of syllabuses and provision within schools and further education. In higher education the sideways shift of polytechnics (now the new universities) has brought higher salaries to senior management, and the dominance of business representation on boards of governors. Other examples include the encouragement of city technology colleges which were originally intended to be largely private sector (business) funded, but have turned out to be private sector led (often explicitly labelled with the name of their business sponsor) but heavily funded by central government. In the field of training the historic involvement of business representatives in the area boards of the Manpower Services Commission and the Training Agency have now culminated in the introduction of Training and Enterprise Councils (TECs), whose operation is largely to be delegated to boards made up of local business leaders. These TECs may also begin to offer the framework for more extensive strategic policy-making at local level, probably with the co-operation of elected local governments, but with little doubt about which are expected to be the lead (or 'enabling') agencies. The setting up of networks of locally-based TECs in England and Wales and Local Enterprise Companies in Scotland is possibly the most direct expression of moves to give an increased role to business in areas previously defined as the responsibility of local government. Although there remains some question about the extent to which business leaders will become actively involved in the running of TECs the structure of political representation on their boards makes it clear whose priorities are intended to dominate. And they have sometimes been used as a platform from which it has been possible to generate pressure for additional funding for locally-based training infrastructure and to raise other local business concerns.

Similarly, although some doubts have been expressed about the adequacy of funding available to TECs, their role as conduit of funds for training to other parts of the public sector reverses the traditional relationship between educationalists and employers (see Peck 1991).

The role of the European Commission in encouraging the development of partnership at local and regional levels should also not be underestimated, although its powers are less direct than those of national government. The existence of EC funds as supplements to local authority income in some areas has encouraged many councils to direct their attention to finding ways of utilizing them (in particular, but not only, trying to draw on the so called structural funds – the European Regional Development Fund for infrastructural spending, and the European Social Fund, for spending on training for the long-term unemployed). Increasing numbers of councils now have European officers whose responsibility it is to co-ordinate relations with the EC and to ensure that the right proposals go to the right parts of the European bureaucracy. The implications of this are two fold: in the first place it effectively encourages local authorities to bypass the institutions of national government and enter into direct negotiation with the EC (even if in the end proposals formally have to pass through the appropriate government ministries); and secondly it reinforces moves towards the development of partnerships at local level because that is specifically encouraged by the EC (see, for example, Lowe's explanation for the reform of the structural funds in the late 1980s, Lowe 1988). The EC now expects proposals for spending from its structural funds to come through Integrated Development Operations (IDOPs), organized at sub-regional level. Instead of considering and approving detailed proposals for specific projects, the intention is that a broad plan is approved for a particular area and that detailed proposals are considered by a committee based in that area, whose membership is drawn from representatives of central government, local government and the private sector. In other words, IDOPs are intended to institutionalize local or regional partnerships (Preston and Hogg 1990). In Britain the first of these arrangements were set up in Strathclyde and South Yorkshire and Humberside in the late 1980s.

As well as the undoubtedly deliberate process of restructuring from above, recently reinforced by the City Challenge initiative, there have been substantial initiatives from business leading to similar conclusions which have ultimately been endorsed by the centre. Business in the Community (BiC), for example, has acted as a crucial focus for business involvement in the development of policies in the inner cities, and a more 'neutral' arena through which collaboration between business and local government could be developed without the high level of political controversy within official politics. Jacobs notes the way in which BiC has set out to create new forms of business leadership in the process of urban economic regeneration, for example, through the formation of Business Leadership Teams, involving senior local businessmen alongside representatives from local government, the trade unions, education and the voluntary sector (Jacobs 1990a and 1992, ch. 9). He suggests that organizations such as BiC 'often seem to be trying to create a climate for business leadership which . . . runs against the grain of Britain's tradition of public municipal provision' (Jacobs 1990b, p. 7).

As we have seen, the discovery of a more explicit political role for capital at local level has not been left to the Marxists, but has been directly espoused by those apparently speaking for capital. It would be difficult to find a more explicit expression of this than the one outlined in a report on 'Leadership in the Community' prepared for Business in the Cities (a joint organization supported by the Confederation of British Industries and BiC). Here too, new structures, new political forms, possibly even new state forms, are identified. The report argues that within a city, 'the division of responsibilities among stake-holders . . . requires a business plan. A city often needs a partnership to function as "Board of Directors" to co-ordinate its "staff", "line" and area activities, just as a business does. The local council cannot bear this responsibility alone' (Bennett and Business in the Community 1990, pp. 12–13). The nature of 'partnership' implies the need to set up an identifiable 'executive power and agency' (ibid., p. 23) separate from elected local governments. The language of business – using the words of the new management – is used as a focus of policy development. Stress is placed on the need to develop 'mission' statements, and business plans, based on SWOT analysis (strengths, weaknesses, opportunities and threats). The new teams are advised to aim for flagship projects, rather than integrated programmes such as those which elected local government is expected to develop. They are exhorted to act like businesses (ibid., pp. 26–9).

But there may still be hope for the strategic managers and those looking to develop the 'enabling authority' since there is also evidence that business needs local government institutions with which to form the all important partnerships. Most business initiatives have themselves explicitly sought to involve local councils, whether as a token of representation for the 'local community' or because it is, in effect, council officers who have played an initiating role. Even the Audit Commission has stressed the need to encourage active co-operation between local government and business in the process of economic development (Audit

Commission 1989b). The balance of power between élites within Britain's urban regimes may have changed, but the membership of those élites has still not changed significantly.

Those speaking for local government often argue that it is only their initiatives and assistance which allow initiatives such as enterprise agencies to survive. Certainly, as Moore and Richardson (1989) note, there has been a substantial growth in partnership models rather than one which implies the possibility of purely private sector initiative. Local authorities have themselves played a major part in helping to create the hybrid organizations which draw business into key areas of local decision-making, offering finance, staff and other support. The new left (local socialist) authorities also played their part (although rarely with encouragement from the centre). Indeed it could be said that they led the way by giving such a high profile to the local economy. The enterprise boards which they set up have easily fitted into the enterprise agency model, themselves suggesting partnership and a new closeness between private and public sectors at local level, and even those authorities such as Sheffield, which avoided the enterprise board model have increasingly emphasized the importance of partnership (see Cochrane 1988, and Totterdill 1989, pp. 514–16). Sheffield's Economic Regeneration Committee, which is made up of representatives of local employers, government agencies, respectable community organizations – such as churches – and trade unions, is a formal expression of this. SERC has taken on a wide strategic role, not only setting out to develop plans for economic regeneration (for example, in plans for the Lower Don Valley, SERC 1987), but also seeking to set out a wider framework for the local politics of development and welfare (SERC 1992). In Sheffield a formal agreement has even been drawn up between the city council and the Sheffield Development Corporation. The organization of the World Student Games (which took place in 1991) was a rather less successful example of collaboration. A joint business/local authority delegation was sent to Zagreb to put the case for giving the games to Sheffield, and a private sector-based organization was initially given the task of raising finance for and organizing the games, although in the end this had to be taken over by the city council since it proved unable to raise the necessary funds. The losses had to be borne by the council. In the context of increased competition between places, local government as local state may still have the responsibility for maintaining the necessary infrastructure. It remains difficult for the private sector to develop a clear unity of purpose without the active intervention of the state in some form.

In Birmingham, too, the city council clearly has played a significant catalytic role, and leading councillors have stressed their desire to make community gain from development, but it is clear that business organizations also see themselves as undertaking strategic planning for urban regeneration. Birmingham Heartlands, for example, has been set up as a private company, 65 per cent owned by five development companies and 35 per cent by the city council. It now has the task of setting out a strategic planning framework, organizing land-pooling and offering other assistance to the consortia which are developing the main projects in a large area of East Birmingham (Carley 1991, pp. 107–9). Carley sums up the relationship positively, concluding that it is 'neither business-led nor public sector-led, but is the result of balanced partnerships between the private sector, often led by the Chamber of Commerce, and the Birmingham City Council' (ibid., p. 114).

The nature and significance of the local politics of business has been debated more extensively in the US, where Logan and Molotch have developed the notion of an 'urban growth machine' as a useful starting point (Molotch 1976, Logan and Molotch 1987). Their approach has explained local politics by focusing on the role of property and development interests primarily concerned with the maximization of income from rent and property values. Smith takes a similar view of the US experience, stressing the extent to which 'public–private partnerships' have generally been oriented towards restoring or increasing 'the property value of urban space' (Smith 1988, p. 43). This interpretation has, however, been sharply criticized by Cox and Mair for being so narrowly focused on property values, to the extent that Logan and Molotch themselves have to acknowledge the role of other groups through a sleight of hand, so that 'rentiers' seem to lose their initially central place in the theory (Cox and Mair 1989, pp. 138–9).

As an alternative, they suggest that urban growth coalitions will be organized between groups and organizations which are, in some sense, locally dependent. The notion of local dependence implies rather more than that people and organizations cannot easily move, but also that they define themselves by (and reproduce themselves in specific ways because of) their particular location (reflected, for example in Harvey's notion of a 'spatial fix'. Harvey 1989b, ch. 5). There may be conflicts between different groups at this level (for example over industrial restructuring, or over environmental issues) and it is because of these, according to Cox and Mair, that business coalitions may develop. These are made up of local firms which 'attempt to ward off opposition to their plans for local economic development by forging a consensus based on the co-optation of their potential opponents, a consensus in which the politics of restructuring is conceived of as a competition among "localities" rather than as a struggle within them' (Cox and Mair 1988, pp. 307–8).

Harvey takes this further by indicating how competition may move beyond the more obvious aspects of local economic development. He argues that, 'The active production of places with special qualities becomes an important stake in spatial competition between localities, cities, regions and nations. Corporatist forms of governance can flourish in such spaces, and themselves take on entrepreneurial roles in the production of favourable business climates and other special qualities. And it is in this context that we can better situate the striving . . . for cities to forge a distinctive image and to create an atmosphere of place and tradition that will act as a lure to both capital and people "of the right sort"' (Harvey 1989a, p. 295). In the US context, Gottdiener concludes that this process means that we have seen the death of local politics, but perhaps it is more accurate to say that we are seeing its transformation along different lines (Gottdiener 1987).

Although the notion of an urban growth coalition (particularly as developed by Cox and Mair and modified in the light of Harvey's arguments) may be a useful one in Britain, too, it has barely been developed in this context. One recent attempt to do so makes little direct reference to the US theories, except by implication, suggesting instead that the key 'coalition' in the development of Swindon was between leading politicians and professionals (Bassett and Harloe 1990, p. 58). And this suggests a continuing problem for the theory in its more general forms: many of the policy features of growth coalitions seem to show themselves even where the active participation of a business coalition or property-based coalition is more difficult to identify. In the case of Britain, as we have seen, it has been necessary to construct business involvement from above. It has not simply been generated as a result of local pressures, from existing business groups. An underlying problem with the theories is that they tend to imply the possibility of straight-forwardly identifying clear (and conflicting) local interests held by different groups. Since, however, these 'interests' only develop in the context of more extensive networks of national politics, political and professional ideologies it may be possible for a local political organization (such as Swindon's Labour leadership) or professional group (such as Swindon's chief officers) to develop a local politics of growth in which – to start with at least – the business interests have to be assumed instead of being an already existing and locally identifiable force. The focus on the local in this context, whilst useful in confirming the possibility of locally-based alliances, which are clearly important in many places, may also make it more difficult to accept the significance of wider national ideologies and political structures. And may imply that the initiative is being taken by groups which, in Britain at least, often look as if they have had to be dragged rather unwillingly into the political arena.

THE RISE OF MANAGEMENT

The increased political importance of business in policy-making at local level goes far beyond direct involvement, which is strongest in the fields most directly relevant to business interests (such as economic development, education and training). The business model has also (as in the late 1960s) been taken as the most appropriate one for the organization of local provision. The importance of popular management texts has been noted by Stoker and others (for example, Lowndes 1990, Smith 1989, Stewart 1992, Stoker 1989a, p. 147). Although these texts clearly are important as a source of rhetoric, because local government professionals increasingly seem to want to define their roles in ways which fit private sector business models, it is less clear how effectively they will be translated into practice. Many key professionals are seeking legitimacy not from the electoral process, but from their ability to fit in with the latest management language, particularly reflected in the shift of usage (admittedly still tentative in many places) from 'client' to 'consumer'. They, too, are beginning to look for value added activities (such as the provision of cable TV in rented housing), and stress the importance of flexibility and marketing. The business orientation is reflected too, of course, in the management buy outs which have taken place in some areas as well as in much of the voluntary sector which is increasingly expected to replace local government as provider. Business is increasingly given formal representation on the boards of various charitable and quasi-charitable organizations, such as housing associations, and their own internal management structures have also often changed to reflect this.

Not all aspects of the local welfare state lend themselves easily to direct business involvement and influence. Nor is it always quite so clear how they relate to the needs of business. It may be a mistake to look too obsessively for connections. The linkages may be rather more subtle, suggesting changes in the dominant common sense or what is taken for granted as much as any direct business involvement. The clearest example of this is probably the way in which the business model has been appropriated within local government for the organization of its own activities – from strategic policy-making and mission statements, down to the making of business plans, the issuing of contracts and the monitoring of service provision. In the 1960s the language of management was utilized to justify expansion, but this time it is being taken up in the context of contraction. The resonance of popular management texts among local government's new managers is perhaps not surprising. Tom Peters' notion of 'Thriving on Chaos' seems to have struck chords with some senior managers in the late 1980s (see, for example, Smith 1989) and Moss Kanter's identification of post-entrepreneurial styles of management appears to offer still more possibilities to a beleaguered public sector (Moss Kanter 1989). Although Hoggett initially identified a crucial role for 'left' politicians and Holliday saw a similar role for politicians of the new suburban right in overcoming bureaucratic conservatism and 'dragging' local government managers into the second half of the twentieth century, that no longer seems necessary (Hoggett 1987, Holliday 1991a). At least some public sector managers seem to be drawing on these approaches to escape from the neo-Taylorist impli- cations of the reforms of the early 1980s with their stress on targets and performance measurement (and considered by Pollitt 1990). Private sector consultancy firms are increasingly being used to give legitimacy both to the internal restructuring of management (see, for example, Holliday 1991a, which records a series of consultancy reports in Kent through the 1980s) and to new forms of political arrangement at local level (see, for instance, the proposals of SERC 1987 for a locally-based arm's-length urban development agency, and Kennedy 1991 which proposes new arrangements for the running of London. Both were the product of consultancies).

Clarke and Newman note the evangelical tone of the new management literature, and it is difficult indeed not to find echoes of this in the new 'visions' and 'strategies' which are proliferating throughout local government with the help of a series of consultancy firms (Clarke and Newman 1992b). This can probably be illustrated well enough with the help of just one example. The 'vision' of Buckinghamshire's Social Services Department is: 'To be the best and give of our best'. And its 'mission' is: 'to enable people who are in need because of disability or vulnerability to achieve, maintain or restore a defined level of social independence or quality of life. It does this by identifying and assessing needs, and by making the best use of available resources to provide access to appropriate individualized services.' Within local government stress is increasingly placed on the need to change existing organizational cultures and the move to managerialism has become a key element in the reshaping of welfare. As Clarke and Newman note: 'Management is the necessary corollary of the dismantling of the familiar structures of bureau-professionalism. Managers are those who "understand" markets; who can extract the untapped potential from the "human resources"; who are sensitized to the "needs of the customer"; who can deliver "results" and who can be relied on to "do the right thing". The unlocking of trade union organization, bureau-professionalism and local political representation requires "management to provide an alternative mode of power" (Clarke and Newman 1992a, p. 8). Pollitt highlights the power of managerialism as an ideology because of the way in which it emphasizes the importance of managers in all organizations, whether in the public or private sectors (Pollitt 1990). Although his own conclusions are rather different, Hoggett's analysis of the new management is also helpful here: 'rather than attempt to strengthen "management" in order to control "professionals" the strategy shifts towards creating managers out of the professionals' (Hoggett 1991, p. 254).

The point here is not to suggest that management is unnecessary in the public sector, but to highlight some of the ways in which notions of management are being used as to change the old ways of running things and to show that these are not just 'neutral' techniques which necessarily improve organizations and the way they operate, but themselves reflect (and reinforce) new sets of power relations. Although it may be dangerous to exaggerate the practical significance of the new management rhetoric, it is increasingly clear that many key professionals seek legitimacy not from the electoral process, but from their ability to fit in with the latest management language, particularly reflected in the shift of usage from 'client' to 'consumer', 'user' or 'customer', as well as a new interest in marketing and in 'quality' (see, for example, LGTB 1987, Stewart and Walsh 1989). The name of the Local Government Training Board (after its merger with the Local Authorities' Conditions of Service Advisory Board) was even changed in 1991 to the Local Government Management Board. The Audit Commission, too, has played an important part in this process, going beyond the early identification of economy, efficiency and effectiveness to the notion of the 'competitive council', which has also been reinterpreted and taken up extensively among local authority managers (Audit Commission 1988). Although the concept of the 'enabling authority' was first developed by politicians seeking to fragment and undermine local government bureaucracies, as we have seen in Chapter 4, it has also been widely utilized by senior managers to justify giving them increased strategic authority and developing new forms of management structure (with themselves at the core), based on private-sector models rather than public-sector hierarchies (Brooke 1989b). As the Department of the Environment consultation paper on the structure of local government recognizes, the response of local government managers to the 'purchaser/provider' distinction has been ambivalent and many with ambitions to take a strategic role would agree that 'The task of setting standards, specifying the work to be done and monitoring performance is done better if it is fully separated from the job of providing the services' (Department of the Environment 1991b, para. 19).

Local government's own writers on management have not been far behind in reinterpreting the new approaches for public sector consumption (see, for example, Clarke and Stewart 1990, Hambleton and Hoggett 1990, Stewart and Walsh 1989). Hoggett has suggested that the spread of the new management will lead to the possibility of post-bureaucratic organization or 'freedom within boundaries' for those working within local government, generally stressing the similarity between public and private sector arrangements (Hoggett 1991, p. 250) Stewart on the other hand has emphasized the necessary differences between public and private sector management, stressing (as we have seen) the necessity of retaining a public service orientation. He argues that, 'To attempt to manage a service in the public sector as if it was in the private sector is bad management because it is management contrary to the distinctive purposes, conditions and tasks of the public sector' (Stewart 1992, p. 28). He emphasizes the extent to which local authorities, like governments, have a range of objectives which may not always be consistent with each other, so that budgets are the outcome of deciding between competing choices, rather than the necessary corollary of a forecast of sales (p. 35). He stresses the need for councils to agree a balance between objectives, and the extent to which this means their policy-making needs to be part of a wider public discourse and systems of public accountability.

In a sense Stewart's arguments represent a warning about the processes of change taking place. They are opposed to the systems of contracting behind closed doors, being monitored by officials. But this is the direction being taken in practice. Council and committee agreement on visions, mission statements and business plans leaves the managers to get on with it, drawing up their individualized assessments. The issuing of contracts impose duties of commercial confidence and forces them to set out a rigid set of requirements whose delivery may then be easily monitored. Paradoxically, despite their force, Stewart's arguments seem more likely to provide a palatable means of introducing the methods of which he is so critical into the local government which he means to defend, precisely because he is so aware of the problems and so sympathetic to the ambitions of professionals concerned about service delivery (see, for example, Clarke and Stewart 1990).

In this round of restructuring, as in the period of modernization discussed in Chapter 1, looking at the experience of social services departments is helpful in highlighting some of the main directions of change. Within the 'enabling' authority, the role of social services departments is seen to be one of managing rather than providing welfare or – to use the language which has increasingly been adopted – care services. Legislation and government guidelines on community care now talk of care managers, rather than social workers (see, for example, HMSO 1988). In the child protection field emphasis is placed on interagency working and collaboration (see, for example, Hallett and Birchall 1992). The key skills are those of assessment, of managing a range of different providers including nominally paid 'volunteer' labour (preparing plans for individual cases) and of working with professionals from a range of other agencies including health authorities, the voluntary sector, schools and the police. In this approach, managing includes the 'human resource management' of a much more complex 'labour force'. The Griffiths report argues strongly for more management training in qualifying and in-service training for social workers to cope with these changed responsibilities (HMSO 1988).

These legislative changes which brought the NHS and Community Care Act 1990 and the Children Act 1989 were the end product of debates which went on through the 1980s, at local and national levels, within policy networks and professional communities as well as in party politics. They were not simply the product of a 'new right' policy agenda as has sometimes been suggested (see, for example, Hudson 1990, who explores some of the contradictions and tensions within the community care proposals, and Frost 1992, who considers the implications of the Children Act as a 'progressive' piece of legislation). There is not a high degree of party political controversy surrounding the legislation itself. Nor – except in terms of the individual responses of social workers having to deal with the changes in local authorities – has there been any significant professionally-based resistance. On the contrary, most professional commentary has been concerned to identify the positive (or 'progressive') points of the legislation and to focus on how it may be used most effectively. This may or may not be an appropriate response to the legislation but it certainly illustrates one of the ways in which managerialism works as an acid with which chains of welfare professionalism may be dissolved, to the extent that welfare professionals themselves seem unable to present an alternative vision.

THE IMPLICATIONS OF FRAGMENTATION

The rise of managerialism fits in with another aspect of making local government more business-like which has involved the redistribution of its responsibilities to a series of different agencies. The old state-run services have increasingly been broken up in moves towards a range of more business-like organizations. Some of these have literally been privatized, although frequently they are almost entirely dependent on contracts from local government. Within local governments, too, this shift has found expression in the creation of direct service organizations. Others may more accurately be described as quasi-local government (or parastatal) organizations. Stoker (1991, ch. 3) discusses the growing number of these, and they are increasingly familiar aspects of the emerging welfare regime. Most obvious, perhaps, has been the dramatic growth in the number of housing associations over the 1980s, many of which have been used by local governments to give them arm's-length control and access to central funds, and almost all of which have been dependent on links to local and central government for survival. Other forms of trust have also begun to emerge, particularly in the South of England, where the 'provider' aspects of welfare have often been trustified – it is not uncommon, for example, to find social services' residential homes for older people reappearing in this guise. In Milton Keynes a trust has even been set up to take on responsibility for much of the parkland bequeathed by the development corporation on its departure in 1992.

Although local authority social services departments are formally given a leading role both in the fields of community care and child protection, in practice the legislation helps to fragment responsibility between agencies, only bringing it together in forms of collaboration and joint working. In community care this has been particularly focused on collaboration between the local authorities and health authorities, but, of course, other agencies have also been involved, from voluntary bodies to the private sector, for example through direct negotiation over residential care with private sector homes. In the field of child protection the growing stress on interagency co-operation changes the position of local government in rather a different way, since it implies that no one agency has the necessary expertise in the area and that the ability to negotiate with others to produce consistent child protection plans is more important than any specific expertise. In both cases managerial rather than professional skills become more highly valued. A recent survey of existing research evidence on the gains of collaborative working in child protection points out that the results are equivocal (Hallett and Birchall

1992, p. 97). But, of course, that's not necessarily the point of the changes.

Another aspect of change to which attention has frequently been drawn is a move towards more decentralized delivery systems. Initiatives of this sort have usually been analysed in terms of their stated aims of increasing democratic involvement in, and increasing the efficiency of service delivery (see, for example, Hoggett and Hambleton 1987). But if they are considered as part of a wider process of state restructuring, then their role may be rather more equivocal. So, for example, 'devolved' budgeting, in which managers (e.g. at team manager level in social services departments, or headteacher level in schools) have been given more responsibility for managing their own budgets (see, for example, Geeson and Haward 1991 on Berkshire). The double-edged nature of such 'devolution' for professionals and (non-strategic) managers in times when budgets are tight will be clear enough, and there is little doubt that devolution has often been used in practice as a means of increasing financial and managerial controls (Flynn 1987). Clarke and Newman draw attention to the extent to which control from the centre may actually become tighter, through complex systems of monitoring and scrutiny, particularly through the use of 'improved' reporting systems made possible by new technology (Clarke and Newman 1992a, pp. 13–14).

Many of the 'democratic' features of decentralization policies within local government seem familiar from earlier attempts at 'community development', encouraging incorporation rather than autonomous action (and which were so heavily criticized by Cockburn 1977). They offer a way of integrating and better managing the troublesome classes left in the residual (means tested) welfare state, as well as the staff who manage them. It is accepted that these groups – including women and black people – need to be given representation within the system, but their position within the hierarchy is clear. This is a point which has been made forcibly even in cases where the avowed intention of politicians and policymakers has been rather different (see, for example, Harriss 1989 on the co-option of members of the women's movement by 'left' councils in the 1980s, and Baker 1991 on some of the problems associated with the appointment of Race Relations Advisers). The key decisions about resources are taken elsewhere, by the strategists, the budget setters and the representatives of other interests. In a two-tier system, there is also likely to be a two-tier corporatism. The fragmentation of the local welfare state helps to confirm these shifts, moving key decision-making into increasingly enclosed arenas, such as the interagency bodies demanded by community care and child protection legislation, even while 'users' are empowered and parents are expected to 'participate' in child protection conferences.

Again the example of 'Sheffield 2000' is interesting here. Stress is placed on notions of 'community empowerment' which is intended to ensure that decision-makers listen, but also effectively shifts responsibility to them and makes it easier (for business and local government) to license particular groups by stressing the extent to which they require financial support. The discussion of collaborative work in Sheffield 2000 indicates that:

> Communities and the voluntary sector need to make links with businesses and other enabling organizations to work in collaboration. The voluntary sector needs to be clear about its role and its limitations to enable effective participation. An initial and pervasive difficulty is the imbalance of power between participants, particularly when community groups work with large and powerful organizations. Powerful agencies will therefore need to resource their less powerful partners for effective participation.
>
> Powerful public and private sector organizations should learn from and be prepared to listen to local communities. Inappropriate and insensitive funding and regeneration projects may neglect the needs of local people and can be destructive. It is important therefore to devise a consultative mechanism where agencies and companies are made accountable to local groups with whom they work. Only through consideration and co-operation can Sheffield fully realize the benefits of social and economic regeneration.
>
> *(SERC, undated, p. 18)*

One of the effects of the changes which have been taking place is to legitimate the concerns of some groups while effectively marginalizing and managing the demands of others. The shifts in forms of political representation have highlighted a new position for business and this has been reinforced by the increased use of management-oriented language in local government. One reflection of this is the way in which trade unions have largely been absorbed into the new organizations as secondary partners – grateful to be involved, but left to argue for the 'greater good' expressed in corporate (business led or influenced) organizations such as Training and Enterprise Councils and other local partnerships. But they have also helped to legitimate a range of 'respectable' voluntary organizations and community groups, some of whom may also be involved in service delivery (including many of the non-business pressure groups identified by Stoker and Wilson 1991, pp. 30–31). At the same time, it is increasingly clear that a wide range of organizations and 'sectional' interests are setting out to make their voices heard at local level, outside the traditional structures of party politics. Gyford writes of 'a proliferation of pressure groups at both local and national level, devoted to the achievement of quite particularized goals in such areas as pollution and the environment, sexual behaviour, media policy, animal welfare, homelessness, transport policy, energy policy and disarmament and defence' (Gyford 1986, p. 109).

The increased fragmentation and diversity at the level of user groups is being met by a response at the centre (or within a range of centres) which seeks to manage diversity in an ideological context which explicitly recognizes the paramount importance of the image of places in the competition for growth and prosperity. Those voluntary organizations which look and operate most like businesses are likely to benefit most from these arrangements, themselves effectively becoming part of the local state and its management, particularly given the overlapping network of representation at management board level. Other smaller community-based organizations, often run by women who are the main users of the services involved (including, for example, play centres, welfare rights groups, community transport organizations and even women's aid centres), are in danger of being so dependent on financial support from councils that they find it hard to retain their autonomy (particularly since funds are only likely to be on offer if a space is made on the management committee for a representative of the council). The old 'clients' of welfare – particularly those who are not organized in any way – are likely to lose what limited power they had, not only through elections, but also because they are no longer able directly to confront councillors over particular issues. If there is a range of community organizations, none of which is perceived as being completely representative (e.g. because their ambitions are 'particularized'), then it will be the task of officers somehow to balance their potentially competing (and possibly contradictory) demands. If most forms of service delivery are the immediate responsibility of other agencies, and councillors are concerned with strategy, rather than individual cases, then it is no longer clear how or where to impose pressure. Becoming a 'customer' (even if your rights are spelled out in a glossy charter) reduces political power (however limited) replacing it with a rule-based quasi-contractual complaints system. As one chief executive (of a Labour authority) explained in interview: contracting out works well, because it means the council itself cannot be blamed, and councillors can stand alongside their electors in blaming those delivering inadequate services. He might have added, even if they cannot always do much about it.

CONCLUSION

It is not necessary to be convinced by Saunders' suggestion that there has been a move from more to less democratic forms of local government within a dual state to acknowledge that it is possible to identify the growth of more 'corporatist' modes of mediation at local level, particularly in the extent of representation of business interests, but possibly also a decline of representation for traditional welfare state professionals (Saunders 1984, p. 35). Although Dunleavy and O'Leary use neo-pluralism to describe arrangements which are not dissimilar (Dunleavy and O'Leary 1987, ch. 5) the new arrangements certainly look more like forms of corporatism – with the functional representation of different groups at local level through a variety of organizations, including, but not exclusively, elected local governments – set within the broader framework of a capitalist political economy. The state continues to play an active role as mediator between different interests, managing those otherwise excluded, but more clearly than ever does so in an overall context which acknowledges the dominance of business. The direction of change is clear enough: if the post-war settlement was one which acknowledged the role of the working class and its organizations, the settlement of the 1980s, arising from the crisis of social democracy which characterized the 1970s, is one which starts from the needs of business and its organizations. It is in that sense that it is possible to identify a move from welfare state to enterprise state.

Chapter Seven

From local government to local state: the impact of restructuring

Few people would want to argue against the view that local government in Britain is and has historically been part of the welfare state, but equally few have bothered to explore the implications of this interpretation. Those who have attempted to do so have generally been sidelined in practice by the mainstream of local government studies, even if the value of their contributions has frequently been acknowledged in principle (see, for example, Cockburn 1977, Dearlove 1979, Saunders 1980 and Dunleavy 1980). In practice, dominant discussions of local government are still wrapped up in mythology about local democracy and infused with the notion that local government is best understood as a local version of central government. Much of the argument of the 1980s which focused on conflicts between central and local government reflected this under-standing, so that the conflict was often portrayed as being between different versions of the democratic mandate, and supporters of local government attempted to produce evidence which showed that councils were more popular than central government and in some sense had more legitimacy in running their own 'communities', while its critics took the view that central government had greater claims to democratic legitimacy (for example, Adam Smith Institute 1989, Duncan and Goodwin 1988, Jones and Stewart 1983). One implication drawn from these debates was that as long as the appropriate framework for community government could be put together then problems would disappear (see, for example, Stewart and Stoker 1988, Young 1986 and Widdicombe Report 1986 more generally).

These arguments are helpful insofar as they highlight the continued importance of local politics and the importance of conflicts over levels of expenditure, so they should not be dismissed out of hand. But if they are allowed to dominate discussion, as they have tended to, then they obscure some of the more important changes which have been taking place. They leave critical commentators cheering from the sidelines for whichever set of politicians or (to use the word generally favoured in local government studies) practitioners they support. Dunleavy has criticized much of the academic writing on local government in the 1960s and 1970s for being written from the point of view of the 'inside dopester', that is based on information drawn from close relationships with political and professional actors, rather than on any attempt to analyse their behaviour: with the role of 'mediating the objective perceptions and valuable insights of local politicians to a wider audience . . . or that of policy advisor, removed from the routines of day-to-day administration, capable of taking a larger view and perhaps versed in a more sophisticated appreciation of democratic theory, but fundamentally concerned with the same goals and operating in the same ideological frame as local government itself' (Dunleavy 1980, p. 7; see also Dearlove's sharp critique 1979, pp. 258–9). This criticism retains much force at the start of the 1990s, in part because the research relationship always encourages researchers to develop sympathy with the concerns of the researched, particularly when they appear to be misunderstood. In this case it is reinforced by the extent to which many of those writing in the field also rely on training and consultancy contracts from those who are being researched. This encourages close relationships which make it difficult to stand back from the agenda as it is understood by existing local governments and – possibly more significant – senior figures within it.

Locating local government explicitly as an integral part of the welfare state, on the other hand, helps to bring out some of the key features of development since 1945, as well as highlighting the ways in which it has been reshaped in the last 25 years. And it also makes it easier to explore and acknowledge some of the tensions between the different roles that it has been expected to play over those years.

The restructuring of the local welfare state in Britain has been the product of a complex series of interactions. It is, however, possible to summarize the main elements of these relatively briefly:

1   Restructuring has taken place in the context of and in response to a wider crisis in the Keynesian welfare state which has stretched out since the mid-1970s. It was clear that the social democratic political arrangements which promised economic prosperity and full employment as the basis on which a welfare state could be provided could no longer be sustained. Economic failure and political failure were closely linked. The analysis of welfare policy in Britain has tended to focus mainly on this crisis and to suggest that the main direction of change has been from this (collectivist, corporatist, even Fordist) form to its opposite (individualist, market-based, post-Fordist) form. One purpose of this paper has been to suggest that such dichotomies are not always very helpful, but the extent and nature of the crisis nevertheless provide an important material and ideological background to the restructuring which is taking place.

2   In large part the increased significance of the local level in the process of restructuring reflects the increased globalization of production, since as firms move beyond the national level, the important aspects of competition are not only between countries (and global regions), but also (and possibly more importantly) between places, where production (of profits as well as services and manufacturing) is actually located. The growing importance of supranational levels of political bargaining (for example through the European Community) which set out the ground rules of localized competition is parallelled by the growing importance of activity at local level (see Commission of the European Communities Directorate General for Regional Policy 1991 for an attempt to link these levels). Some (such as Cooke 1990) argue that this creates new opportunities for political proactivity at local level, but others are more sceptical (Cox and Mair 1991, Harvey 1989b, Ch. 5) suggesting that local politicians have limited room for manoeuvre, since they have to please the businesses they wish to attract or retain, which means that their political agendas are largely determined by others. The arguments of this book are rather closer to those of the sceptics.

3   Many of the direct pressures for change within Britain have come from above: from initiatives sponsored by central government, particularly inspired by 'Thatcherism' and the ideas of the 'new right'. The key features here have been (a) attempts to reduce spending on welfare, helping to create a permanently beleaguered atmosphere of

managing cuts within the local state (in the early 1990s these pressures seem to have increased with far-reaching cuts threatened throughout local government); (b) shifts in forms of provision, through attempts to create surrogate markets, for example in the forms of privatization, compulsory competitive tendering, the purchaser/provider split, fragmentation of providers, the removal of some forms of activity from local government responsibility, etc; (c) attempts to encourage business involvement in the civic arena (for example, through TECs, Urban Development Corporations, City Challenge, support for enterprise agencies, direct involvement in agencies through boards of governors, etc.).

4   But – as we have seen – the changes have not simply involved the working out of a new right agenda. Business interests have set out to determine the welfare agenda at local as well as national level, through Business in the Community, the Confederation of British Industry, and the work of Chambers of Commerce (expressed, for example, in Bennett and Business in the Community 1990, and Bennett 1991; see also Jacobs 1992, ch. 9). At local level individuals identified as the 'movers and shakers' of the business community (see, for example, Fogarty and Christie 1990, p. 94) have taken on the role of helping to shape this agenda, with the co-operation of the institutions of central and local government and, frequently, with 'messianic zeal' (Fogarty and Christie 1990, p. 91). Moody has helpfully developed the notion of a 'business agenda' in the US context, stressing that it does not imply agreement on economic theory or on particular policies, but, instead, provides goals which 'allow of some variation in actual implementation, but which . . .[are] precise enough to represent a clear break with liberal or even centrist versions of Keynesian inspired policy' (Moody 1987, p. 154). Jessop has noted the way in which the division between private economy and the state means that the latter remains dependent on the private sector as the source of economic well-being (Jessop 1990, pp. 178–80). It is this dependence in the context of increased competition between places which helps to give the 'business agenda' its powerful resonance at local level, particularly as it stretches beyond the narrow confines of economic policy to reshape welfare regimes.

5   Meanwhile these changes have been reinforced by a more subtle form of shift in agenda, as actors within the state have begun (albeit in crab-like fashion with frequent expressions of concern about the importance of maintaining professional standards) to take on a rather different understanding of their role. Strategic managers have begun to make increasing claims to higher status. They have increasingly

moved away from the notion of local welfare state as self-sufficient provider to that of local government as 'enabler' which – in principle at least – allows them to have a much greater influence as well as giving them a status closer to that of the private sector managers on whom they increasingly base themselves. However illusory their hopes may turn out to be in the harsh light of the 1990s, they present themselves as being at the centre of complex networks of influence. They alone, it is argued (see, for example, Brooke 1989a and b, LGTB 1988, Stewart 1989b), have the potential to embody the overall interests of their areas (and 'communities') and so to manage the contributions of a range of agencies and interests to achieve the best possible welfare outcomes. Senior managers in local government (and chief executives, in particular) are now able to claim a powerful role with a higher status than that of the welfare professionals they have had to manage. The link between these changes and the business agenda is made easier by the way in which managerialism has become the evangelism of the new age, linking private and public sectors, and helping to erode the older hierarchies of welfarism, while replacing them with new and apparently equally unchallengeable hierarchies. The increased use of consultancy organizations to provide advice on management and organizational restructuring is just another example of this.

6   In one sense welfare provision has become more integrated, poten- tially managed more centrally through a network with strategic managers at the core (or in multiple cores linked through forms of interagency working, in which the dominant partner may vary over time). But this has also been accompanied by an increasing insti- tutional fragmentation, characterized by the growth of a multiplicity of providers of one sort or another – from housing associations to health service trusts, from locally managed and grant-maintained schools to training and enterprise councils, from not-for-profit welfare agencies providing residential care to enterprise agencies. State expenditure is increasingly being channelled back to the private sector through contracting out. Although this was originally most obvious for activities such as street cleaning, refuse disposal and housing maintenance, it is inexorably spreading into other areas such as residential care, casualized social work services and even architec- tural services. In practice in the longer term this is likely to make local government, and other parts of the local state which are similarly reliant on contracting out, dependent on a limited range of large national and multinational companies for some aspects of service

provision, and it also helps to reinforce approaches which legitimate business rather than welfare.

For a time in the mid-1970s, discussions of local government were frequently preceded by a ritual statement which emphasized that what was really being discussed was the 'local state', which was a set of social relations, rather than a set of institutions. Having made this clear at the start, in practice the term local state tended to be used simply to mean local government. Rhodes points out that the terms began to be used interchangeably to the extent that using the term 'local state' came to be little more than a sign that the author concerned saw her or himself as writing from a neo-Marxist or neo-Weberian perspective, even when the implications of this for the analysis were by no means clear (Rhodes 1988, pp. 97–8). Not surprisingly, perhaps, as a result the use of the term local state has become less common – writers such as Rhodes and Stoker (1988) explicitly avoid it and even Marxists such as Harvey seem to prefer terms such as 'urban governance' (Harvey 1989c). Despite its absence from much recent literature, however, the value of the distinction between local government and local state is now becoming clearer – indeed it is probably clearer now than it ever was in the high days of its usage in the 1970s. Not only has there been a mushroom growth of local state institutions which are not part of (or are only loosely related to) elected local governments, but also the ways in which some of these institutions express class and other social relations is also often rather more transparent.

Some of the main features of the new world are becoming easier to recognize, but how should the new politics of local government – the newly dominant form of urban regime – be characterized? The notion of 'local corporatism' is a useful starting point in that it highlights the ways in which particular groups are licensed – for example, business groups and the new managers within the state system, but also some other locally-based (community) groups and non-statutory organizations. The dominance of some groups rather than others is perhaps more explicit in these arrangements than in the more classic tripartite forms of corporatism, but the implications are similar, with the ambition of creating an unchallengeable (if still contested) set of aims characterized by consensus on a business-led agenda at local level. Although Schmitter (1989, p. 65) notes that in practice it is impossible to find a 'perfect' corporatism its main features have been summarized frequently enough, at least in ideal typical terms, and it is possible to recognize corporatist features or tendencies when they are there. Cawson defines it comprehensively as a 'process in which organizations representing monopolistic functional interests engage in political exchange with state agencies over public policy outputs which involve those organizations in a role that combines interest representation and policy implementation through delegated self-enforcement' (Cawson 1985b, p. 8). But the value of corporatist formulations is that they direct our attention to the extent to which, in Offe's words, public status is accorded to particular interest groups going beyond the limits of class organizations although – as he also points out – there is an asymmetry in corporatist arrangements which ensures that they place more limitations on labour and other non-capitalist interests than they do on the operations of capital (Offe 1981, pp. 146–50).

It has increasingly been recognized that formulations which focus solely on national level bargaining capital, labour and the state (or other 'peak' organizations) may miss the significance of related arrangements at other levels, whether sectorally or territorially divided (what Cawson calls middle level or 'meso-corporatism' (Cawson 1985a)). They may also miss supranational arrangements such as those associated with the European Community. This is likely to be still more important now that local forms of political accommodation are increasing in importance. Although, in practice, much of the writing on corporatism has focused on direct state–industry relations, such a focus is by no means essential. Cawson has analysed the structures of the welfare state with the help of corporatist theory (Cawson 1982) and Reade's analysis of the planning profession discusses town planners, in ways compatible with the definition cited earlier, as representing a functional interest with special access to power (Reade 1987, pp. 120–31). Rhodes' approach to the analysis of central–local relations, too, may be compatible with some notions of corporatism (even if he continues to favour more pluralist interpretations), because of the way in which he stresses that, 'the professions become institutional-ized in policy networks and their unified view of the world – based on common ideas, values and knowledge – sets the parameters to local decision-making' (Rhodes 1986, p. 241). Although some have been reluctant to utilize the term (see, for example, Brindley *et al.* 1989, Moore and Richardson 1989), the importance of links between business and the state at local level have also increasingly been recognized, and analysis has begun to point to ways in which these links may be understood as both local and corporatist (see, for example, Flynn 1983, Hernes and Selvik 1981, King 1985; Simmie and French 1989). Smith explicitly concludes that the growing numbers of 'public–private partnerships' in the US are 'forms of local corporatism' intended to 'extract material resources from society and to build symbolic support for the goals of local networks of economic and political élites' (Smith 1988, p. 209).

The words used to characterize the new arrangements matter less than understanding the main directions of change. And it is also important to recognize that identifying dominant arrangements as 'corporatist' (or, indeed, 'post-Fordist') is not the end of the matter, because one feature of urban regimes in the 1990s is precisely that they will vary significantly across the country. Indeed there may be more similarities across national boundaries between the ways in which different places govern themselves and are governed than there are within countries, even if the institutional framework appears to be significantly different (this may even lead to the development of cross-boundary networks of alliances between places which share the same interests. The possibility of strategic alliances between cities is discussed in Commission of the European Communities Directorate-General for Regional Policy 1991, pp. 148–9). Within Britain, therefore, it will be necessary to explore more carefully the precise balance between key interests in different places, within the broader constraints of political restructuring. Describing a set of arrangements as corporatist does not mean that the same groups will always be politically dominant in every locality. There may be divisions between local business communities (for example, between those seeking to benefit from property development and existing manufacturing or even commercial interests); there may be places where networks of interests are dominated by professionals within state organizations and others where leaders of political parties take the lead; it may be possible to find places (particularly in the suburbs and Home Counties) where anti-growth coalitions, are strong enough to resist pressures for growth for a time (arguably, of course, it is precisely the easy access to such places which makes neighbouring urban areas 'attractive' to managers and so to investment). The overall tendency may be towards making Britain's local welfare state work better for business, but the ways in which this is achieved will vary markedly, producing a mosaic of local forms rather than one which could be produced from a single universal template.

The local government reforms so far proposed for the 1990s – which point towards the creation of unitary authorities based around recogniz-able localities and the possibility of elected mayor models or others based around a strong executive – make these arguments more rather than less important for two reasons. Firstly, they imply the recognition that local government needs to be restructured in ways which make it easier to construct locally-based partnerships and competition between places, and they suggest moves away from local (in some sense still community-based) councillors towards strategic politicians, more clearly part of the management structure. Secondly, contrary to the hopes of many local politicians up and down the country, the reforms will not bring the devolution of a great deal more power to district councils. Instead, as the changes already introduced in Wales confirm, they reflect a recognition that elected councils are unlikely to retain enough status to justify their current organizational forms. From the point of view of the local managers, the danger is that the reforms will not bring the power and responsibility of the old counties down to district level or to new unitary authorities, but instead simply remove most of those responsibilities to other specialist agencies and leave the rump with the new authorities. Many of the institutions of local government are likely to survive into the 1990s, but their significance will be substantially reduced. It will no longer be possible to equate local politics with the politics of local government, since many of the most important decisions will be taken in quite different forums. And it will only be possible to understand the politics of local government within a wider framework of local politics and the local state.

The position of elected local governments within the changing local political regimes is not a straightforward one. The changes herald neither the necessary 'end' of local government nor the inevitable rise of the 'enabling' authority. But they do imply a rather different role as one (not necessarily leading) element within a more fragmented local state. This means – following the arguments of those who support the notion of the 'enabling' authority – that if elected councils are to retain a significant role then they need to become more rather than less political. Such a conclusion, however, suggests that this cannot be left to the strategic managers seeking to encourage the rational ordering of 'chaos' through the managing of networks from a position of power. Instead it implies the need for councils more explicitly to find ways of reinforcing their democratic legitimacy, actively campaigning at local level and setting out to build community support. That is not something which can simply be taken for granted as arising from the electoral process. On that basis – alongside the recognition that councils are no longer necessarily the dominant political actors at local level – it will be possible to begin to negotiate with others and potentially to build strategic alliances capable of reflecting community needs in all their new complexity, and capable of challenging some of the assumptions which are too often simply taken for granted within the new arrangements.

References

Adam Smith Institute (1989) *Wiser Counsels: The Reform of Local Government*. London: Adam Smith Institute.

Addison, P. (1975) *The Road to 1945: British Politics and the Second World War*. London: Jonathon Cape.

Aglietta, M. (1979) *A Theory of Capitalist Regulation*. London: New Left Books.

Alexander, A. (1991) 'Managing fragmentation – democracy, accountability and the future of local government' *Local Government Studies*, 17(6), 63–76.

Allen, I. (ed.) (1991) *Health and Social Services: The New Relationship*. London: Policy Studies Institute.

Allen, J. (1988) 'The geographies of service', in Massey, D. and Allen J. (eds) *Uneven Re-Development: Cities and Regions in Transition*. London: Hodder and Stoughton.

Allen, J. and Massey, D. (eds) (1988) *The Economy in Question*. London: Sage.

Amin, A. (1989) 'Flexible specialisation and small firms in Italy' *Antipode*, 12(1), 13–34.

Anderson, J. and Ricci, M. (eds) (1990) *Society and Social Science: A Reader*. Milton Keynes: The Open University.

Ascher, K. (1987) *The Politics of Privatisation: Contracting out Public Services.* London: Macmillan.

Audit Commission (1984) *The Impact on Local Authorities' Economy, Efficiency and Effectiveness of the Block Grant Distribution System.* London: HMSO.

Audit Commission (1986) *Making a Reality of Community Care.* London: HMSO.

Audit Commission (1988) *The Competitive Council.* Management Paper No. 1. London: HMSO.

Audit Commission (1989a) *Losing an Empire, Finding a Role.* London: HMSO.

Audit Commission (1989b) *Urban Regeneration and Economic Development: The Local Government Dimension.* London: HMSO.

Audit Commission (1990) *The Administration of the Community Charge.* London: HMSO.

Bagguley, P. (1992) 'Prisoners of the Beveridge dream? The political mobilization of the poor against contemporary welfare regimes.' Paper presented to *Towards a Post-Fordist Welfare State?* Conference, University of Teesside, 17–18 September.

Bailey, S. (1991) 'Fiscal stress: the new system of local government finance in England' *Urban Studies,* 28(6), 889–907.

Bains Report (1972) *The New Local Authorities: Management and Structure, Report of the Study Group on Local Authority Management Structures.* London: HMSO.

Baker, J. (1991) 'Is there a future for local authority race relations advisers?' *Policy and Politics,* 19(3), 167–76.

Bartlett, W. (1991) 'Quasi-markets and contracts: a market and hierarchies perspective on NHS reform' *Studies in Decentralisation and Quasi-Markets 3.* Bristol: School for Advanced Urban Studies.

Bassett, K. and Harloe, M. (1990) 'Swindon: the rise and decline of a growth coalition', in Harloe, M. et al. (eds) *Place, Policy and Politics.* London: Unwin Hyman.

Batley, R. and Stoker, G. (eds) (1991) *Local Government in Europe: Trends and Developments.* London: Macmillan.

Beer, S. (1982) *Britain Against Itself: The Political Contradictions of Collectivism.* London: Faber and Faber.

Benington, J. (1976) *Local Government becomes Big Business.* London: Community Development Project.

Bennett, R. (1991) *British Chambers of Commerce and Industry: Developing a National Network.* London: Association of British Chambers of Commerce.

Bennett, R. and Business in the Community (1990) *Leadership in the Community: A Blueprint for Business Involvement in the 1990s.* London: Business in the Community.

Bennett, R. J. and Krebs, G. (1991) *Local Economic Development: Public–Private Partnership Initiation in Britain and Germany.* London: Belhaven Press.

Berger, S., Hirschman, A. and Maier, C. (1981) *Organizing Interests in Western Europe: Pluralism, Corporatism, and the Transformation of Politics.* Cambridge: Cambridge University Press.

Beveridge, W. (1942) *Social Insurance and Allied Services* Cmd 6404. London: HMSO.

Blunkett, D. and Jackson, K. (1987) *Democracy in Crisis: The Town Halls Respond.* London: The Hogarth Press.

Boddy, M. and Fudge, C. (1984a) 'Labour councils and new left alternatives', in Boddy, M. and Fudge, C. (eds) *Local Socialism? Labour Councils and New Left Alternatives.* London: Macmillan.

Boddy, M. and Fudge, C. (eds) (1984b) *Local Socialism? Labour Councils and New Left Alternatives.* London: Macmillan.

Brake, M. and Hale, C. (1992) *Public Order and Private Lives. The Politics of Law and Order.* London: Routledge.

Branson, N. (1979) *Poplarism 1919–1925: George Lansbury and the Councillors' Revolt.* London: Lawrence and Wishart.

Brett, E. A. (1986) *The World Economy Since the War: The Politics of Uneven Development.* London: Macmillan.

Brindley, T., Rydin, Y. and Stoker, G. (1989) *Remaking Planning: The Politics of Urban Change in the Thatcher Years.* London: Unwin Hyman.

Brooke, R. (1989a) 'The enabling authority – practical consequences' *Local Government Studies*, 15(5), 55–63.

Brooke, R. (1989b) *Managing the Enabling Authority.* London: Longman.

Bulpitt, J. (1983) *Territory and Power in the United Kingdom: An Interpretation.* Manchester: Manchester University Press.

Bulpitt, J. (1989) 'Walking back to happiness? Conservative Party governments and elected local authorities in the 1980s', in Crouch, C. and Marquand, D. (eds) *The New Centralism.* Oxford: *The Political Quarterly*, Blackwell.

Burgess, T. and Travers, T. (1980) *Ten Billion Pounds: Whitehall's Takeover of the Town Halls.* London: Grant McIntyre.

Burns, D. (1992) *Poll Tax Rebellion.* Stirling: A.K.

Burns, W. (1980) *Review of Local Authority Assistance to Industry and Commerce.* Report of the Joint Group of Officials of Local Authority Associations and Government Departments (under the chairmanship of W. Burns). London: Department of the Environment.

Butcher, H., Law, I., Leach, R. and Mullard, M. (1990) *Local Government and Thatcherism.* London: Routledge.

Butler, E. and Pirie, M. (eds) (1981) *Economy and Local Government.* London: Adam Smith Institute.

Campbell, B. (1987) 'Labour's left councils: charge of the light brigade' *Marxism Today*, February.

Campbell, M. (ed.) (1990) *Local Economic Policy.* London: Cassell.

Carley, M. (1991) 'Business in urban regeneration partnerships: a case study in Birmingham' *Local Economy*, 6(2), 100–15.

Carter, P., Jeffs, T. and Smith, M. (eds) (1992) *Changing Social Work and Welfare*. Buckingham: Open University Press.

Cawson, A. (1982) *Corporatism and Welfare*. London: Heinemann.

Cawson, A. (ed.) (1985a) *Organised Interests and the State: Studies in Meso-Corporatism*. London: Sage.

Cawson, A. (1985b) 'Varieties of corporatism: the importance of the meso-level of interest intermediation', in Cawson, A. (ed.) *Organised Interests and the State*. London: Sage.

Central Statistical Office (1991) *United Kingdom National Accounts*. London: HMSO.

Central Statistical Office (1992) *Social Trends 22*. London: HMSO.

Clarke, A. and Cochrane, A. (1989) 'Inside the machine: the left and finance professionals in local government' *Capital and Class*, 37, 35–61.

Clarke, J. and Newman, J. (1992a) 'Managing to survive: dilemmas of changing organisational forms in the public sector', paper presented to the Social Policy Association Conference, Nottingham.

Clarke, J. and Newman, J. (1992b) *The right to manage: a second managerial revolution?* Mimeo.

Clarke, M. and Stewart, J. (1988) *The Enabling Council*. Luton: Local Government Training Board.

Clarke, M. and Stewart, J. (1990) *Developing Effective Public Service Management*. Luton: Local Government Training Board.

Clarke, M. and Stewart, J. (1991) *Choices for Local Government for the 1990s and Beyond*. London: Longman.

Coates, D. (1991) *Running the Country*. Sevenoaks: Hodder and Stoughton.

Cochrane, A. (1986a) 'Community politics and democracy', in Held, D. and Politt, C. (eds) *New Forms of Democracy*. London: Sage.

Cochrane, A. (1986b) 'Local employment initiatives: towards a new municipal socialism?' in Lawless, P. and Raban, C. (eds) *The Contemporary British City*. London: Harper and Row.

Cochrane, A. (1988) 'In and against the market? The development of socialist economic strategies in Britain, 1981–1986' *Policy and Politics*, 16(3), 159–68.

Cochrane, A. (1989) 'Restructuring the state: the case of local government', in Cochrane, A. and Anderson, J. (eds) *Politics in Transition*. London: Sage.

Cochrane, A. (1991) 'The changing state of local government: restructuring for the 1990s' *Public Administration*, 69(3), 281–302.

Cochrane, A. (1993) 'The problem of poverty', in Dallos, R. and McLaughlin, E. (eds) *Social Problems and the Family*. London: Sage.

Cochrane, A. and Anderson, J. (eds) (1989) *Politics in Transition*. London: Sage.

Cockburn, C. (1977) *The Local State: Management of Cities and People*. London: Pluto Press.

Commission of the European Communities Directorate General for Regional Policy (1991) *Europe 2000. Outlook for the Development of the*

Community's Territory. Luxembourg: Office for Official Publications of the European Communities.

Comptroller and Auditor General (1990) *Privatisation of Work in New Town Bodies in England*. London: HMSO.

Cooke, P. (ed.) (1989a) *Localities: The Changing Face of Urban Britain*. London: Unwin Hyman.

Cooke, P. (1989b) 'Locality, economic restructuring and world development', in Cooke, P. (ed.) *Localities*. London: Unwin Hyman.

Cooke, P. (1990) *Back to the Future?* London: Unwin Hyman.

Cowen, H. (1990) 'Regency icons: marketing Cheltenham's built environment', in Harloe, M. *et al.* (eds) *Place, Policy and Politics*. London: Unwin Hyman.

Cox, K. and Mair, A. (1988) 'Locality and community in the politics of local economic development' *Annals of the Association of American Geographers*, 72(2), 307–25.

Cox, K. and Mair, A. (1989) 'Urban growth machines and the politics of local economic development' *International Journal of Urban and Regional Development*, 13(1), 137–46.

Cox, K. and Mair, A. (1991) 'From localised social structures to localities as agents' *Environment and Planning A*, 23(2), 155–308.

Crosland, S. (1983) *Tony Crosland*. London: Coronet.

Crouch, C. and Marquand, D. (eds) (1989) *The New Centralism: Britain out of Step in Europe?* Oxford: The Political Quarterly/Blackwell.

Dallos, R. and McLaughlin, E. (eds) (1983) *Social Problems and the Family*. London: Sage.

Dearlove, J. (1979) *The Reorganisation of Local Government: Old Orthodoxies and a Political Perspective*. Cambridge: Cambridge University Press.

Dearlove, J. and Saunders, P. (1984) *Introduction to British Politics*. Cambridge: Polity Press.

Deem, R., Brehony, K. and Hemmings, S. (1992) 'Social justice, social divisions and the governing of schools', in Gill, D., Mayor, B. and Blair, M. (eds) *Racism and Education. Structures and Strategies*. London: Sage.

Department of the Environment (1991a) *Local Government Finance Statistics: England: Number 2*. London: HMSO.

Department of the Environment (1991b) *The Structure of Local Government in England: A Consultation Paper*. London: HMSO.

Department of the Environment (1992) *Local Government Finance Statistics: England: No. 3*. London: HMSO.

Department of the Environment/Welsh Office (1983) *Rates: Proposals for the Limitation and Reform of the Rating System*, Cmnd 9008. London: HMSO.

Duncan, S. (1989) 'What is locality?' in Peet, R. and Thrift, N. (eds) *New models in Geography, Volume 2*. London: Unwin Hyman.

Duncan, S. and Goodwin, M. (1982) 'The local state: functionalism autonomy and class relations' in Cockburn and Saunders' *Political Geography Quarterly*, 1(1), 77–96.

Duncan, S. and Goodwin, M. (1988) *The Local State and Uneven Development*. Cambridge: Polity Press.

Dunleavy, P. (1980) *Urban Political Analysis*. London: Macmillan.

Dunleavy, P. (1981) 'Perspectives on urban studies', in Blowers, A. *et al.* (eds) *Urban Change and Conflict: An Interdisciplinary Reader*. London: Harper and Row.

Dunleavy, P. (1984) 'The limits to local government', in Boddy, M. and Fudge, C. (eds) *Local Socialism? Labour Councils and New Left Alternatives*. London: Macmillan.

Dunleavy, P. (1985) 'Bureaucrats, budgets and the growth of the state' *British Journal of Political Science*, 15, 299–328.

Dunleavy, P. (1986) 'Explaining the privatisation boom: public choice versus radical explanations' *Public Administration*, 64(1), 13–34.

Dunleavy, P. (1991) *Democracy, Bureaucracy and Public Choice: Economic Explanations in Political Science*. Hemel Hempstead: Harvester Wheatsheaf.

Dunleavy, P. and O'Leary, B. (1987) *Theories of the State: The Politics of Liberal Democracy*. London: Macmillan.

Elam, M. (1990) 'Puzzling out the post-Fordist debate; technology, markets and institutions' *Economic and Industrial Democracy*, 11(1), 9–37.

Evandrou, M., Falkingham, J. and Glennerster, H. (1990) 'The personal social services: "Everybody's poor relation but nobody's baby"', in Hills, J. (ed.) *The State of Welfare*. Oxford: Clarendon Press.

Fleming, A. (1989) Employment in public and private sectors *Economic Trends*, 434, 91–3.

Flynn, N. (1987) 'Delegated financial responsibility and policy-making within social services departments' *Public Money*, 6(4), 41–4.

Flynn, R. (1983) 'Co-optation and strategic planning in the local state', in King, R. (ed.) *Capital and Politics*. London: Routledge & Kegan Paul.

Fogarty, M. and Christie, I. (1990) *Companies and Communities: Promoting Business Involvement in the Community*. London: PSI Publishing.

Foot, M. (1973) *Aneurin Bevan: Vol 2. 1945–1960*. London: Davis-Poynter (page references to Paladin paperback edn, 1975).

Forsyth, M. (1981) *Re-Servicing Britain*. London: Adam Smith Institute.

Fraser, D. (1976) *Urban Politics in Victorian England*. Leicester: Leicester University Press.

Freeman, C. (1987) *Technology Policy and Economic Performance: Lessons from Japan*. London: Pinter.

Freeman, C. and Perez, C. (1988) 'Structural crises of adjustment, business cycles and investment behaviour, in Dosi, G. (ed.) *Technical Change and Economic Theory*. London: Pinter.

Frost, N. (1992) 'Implementing the Children Act 1989 in a hostile climate', in Carter, P. *et al.* (eds) *Changing Social Work and Welfare*. Buckingham: Open University Press.

Gamble, A. (1985) *Britain in Decline: Economic Policy, Political Strategy and the British State*, 2nd edn. London: Macmillan.

Gamble, A. (1988) *The Free Economy and the Strong State*. London: Macmillan.

Geddes, M. (1988) 'The capitalist state and the local economy: "restructuring for labour and beyond"' *Capital and Class*, 35, 85–120.

Geeson, T. and Haward, J. (1990) 'Devolved management – the Berkshire experience' *Local Government Studies*, 16(1), 1–9.

Gibson, J. (1990) *The Politics and Economics of the Poll Tax: Mrs Thatcher's Downfall*. Warley: EMAS Ltd.

Gilroy, P. (1987) *There Ain't No Black in the Union Jack*. London: Hutchinson.

Glennerster, H., Power, A. and Travers, T. (1991) 'A new era for social policy: a new enlightenment or a new leviathan?' *Journal of Social Policy*, 20(3), 389–414.

Goldsmith, M. (1986) 'Managing the periphery in a period of fiscal stress', in Goldsmith, M. (ed.) *New Research in Central–Local Relations*. Aldershot: Gower.

Goldsmith, M. and Villadsen, S. (eds) (1986) *Urban Political Theory and the Management of Fiscal Stress*. Aldershot: Gower.

Goss, S. (1988) *Local Labour and Local Government: A Study of Changing Interests, Politics and Policy in Southwark, 1919 to 1982*. Edinburgh: Edinburgh University Press.

Gottdiener, M. (1987) *The Decline of Urban Politics: Political Theory and the Crisis of the Local State*, Sage Library of Social Research, Vol. 162. London: Sage.

Gough, I. (1979) *The Political Economy of the Welfare State*. London: Macmillan.

Grant, W. (ed.) (1985) *The Political Economy of Corporatism*. London: Macmillan.

Grant, W. and Sargent, J. (1987) *Business and Politics in Britain*. London: Macmillan.

Green, D. (1985) 'From socialism to the new liberalism', in Selsdon, A. (ed.) *The 'New Right' Enlightenment*. London: Economic and Literary Books.

Green, G. (1987) 'The new municipal socialism', in Loney, M. et al. (eds) *The State of the Market*. London: Sage.

Greenwood, R. and Stewart, J. (1974) *Corporate Planning in English Local Government*. London: Charles Knight.

Greer, S., Hedlund, R. and Gibson, J. (eds) (1979) *Accountability in Urban Society: Public Agencies under Fire*, Urban Affairs Annual Reviews, Vol. 15. London: Sage.

Griffiths, Sir R. (1988) *Community Care: Agenda for Action. A Report to the Secretary of State for Social Services*. London: HMSO.

Gurr, T. and King, D. (1987) *The State and the City*. London: Macmillan.

Gutch, R. and Young, K. (1988) *Partners or Rivals? A Discussion Paper on the Relationship between Local Government and the Voluntary Sector*. Luton: Local Government Training Board.

Gyford, J. (1985) *The Politics of Local Socialism*. London: Allen and Unwin.

Gyford, J. (1986) 'Diversity, sectionalism and local democracy', in Widdicombe Report, Research Volume IV, *Aspects of Local Democracy*.

Gyford, J. (1991) *Citizens, Consumers and Councils*. London: Macmillan.

Gyford, J., Leach, S. and Game, C. (1989) *The Changing Politics of Local Government*. London: Unwin Hyman.

Hadley, R. and Hatch, S. (1981) *Social Welfare and the Failure of the State: Centralised Social Services and Participatory Alternatives*. London: Allen and Unwin.

Hakim, C. (1988) 'Self-employment in Britain: recent trends and current issues' *Work, Employment and Society*, 2(4), 421–50.

Hall, S. and Jacques, M. (eds) (1989) *New Times: The Changing Face of Politics in the 1990s*. London: Lawrence and Wishart.

Hallett, C. and Birchall, E. (1992) *Co-ordination and Child Protection: A Review of the Literature*. Edinburgh: HMSO.

Hambleton, R. (1990) 'Urban Government in the 1990s: Lessons from the USA' *Occasional Paper No 35*. Bristol: School for Advanced Urban Studies.

Hambleton, R. and Hoggett, P. (1987) 'Beyond bureaucratic paternalism', in Hoggett, P. and Hambleton, R. (eds) 'Decentralisation and democracy', *Occasional Paper 28*. Bristol: School for Advanced Urban Studies.

Hambleton, R. and Hoggett, P. (1990) 'Beyond Excellence: Quality Local Government in the 1990s' *Working Paper 85*. School for Advanced Urban Studies. (A collection of articles originally published in *Local Government Chronicle* in 1990.)

Hambleton, R., Hoggett, P. and Tolan, F. (1989) 'The decentralisation of public services – a research agenda' *Local Government Studies*, 15(1), 39–56.

Hamnett, C. (1992) 'Running housing: housing policy and the British housing system' Unit 9 of D212, *Running the Country*. Milton Keynes: Open University Educational Enterprises.

Harding, A. (1990) 'Public–private partnerships in urban regeneration', in Campbell, M. (ed.) *Local Economic Policy*. London: Cassell.

Harloe, M., Pickvance, C. and Urry, J. (eds) (1990) *Place, Policy and Politics; Do Localities Matter?* London: Unwin Hyman.

Harris, L. (1988) 'The UK economy at a crossroads', in Allen, J. and Massey, D. (eds) *The Economy in Question*. London: Sage.

Harriss, K. (1989) 'New alliances: socialist-feminism in the Eighties' *Feminist Review*, 31, 34–54.

Harvey, D. (1989a) *The Condition of Postmodernity: An Enquiry into the Origins of Cultural Change*. Oxford: Blackwell.

Harvey, D. (1989b) *The Urban Experience*. Oxford: Blackwell.

Harvey, D. (1989c) 'From managerialism to entrepreneurialism: the transformation in urban governance in late capitalism' *Geografiska Annaler*, 71b, 1: 3–17.

Held, D. and Pollitt, C. (eds) (1986) *New Forms of Democracy*. London: Sage.

Hernes, G. and Selvik, A. (1981) 'Local corporatism', in Berger, S. *et al.* (eds) *Organizing Interests in Western Europe*. Cambridge: Cambridge University Press.

Hill, D. (1970) *Participating in Local Affairs*. Harmondsworth: Penguin.

Hills, J. (ed.) (1990) *The State of Welfare: The Welfare State in Britain since 1974*. Oxford: Clarendon Press.

Hills, J. and Mullings, B. (1990) 'Housing: a decent home for all at a price within their means?' in Hills, J. (ed.) *The State of Welfare*. Oxford: Clarendon Press.

Hirst, P. (1989) 'After Henry', in Hall, S. and Jacques, M. (eds) *New Times*. London: Lawrence and Wishart.

HMSO (1970) *Reform of Local Government in England*, Cmnd 4276. London: HMSO.

HMSO (1986) *Paying for Local Government*, Cmnd 9714. London: HMSO.

Hoggett, P. (1987) 'A farewell to mass production? Decentralisation as an emergent private and public sector paradigm', in Hoggett, P. and Hambleton, R. (eds) 'Decentralisation and democracy', *Occasional Paper 28*. Bristol: School for Advanced Urban Studies.

Hoggett, P. (1990) 'Modernisation, Political Strategy and the Welfare State: An Organisational Perspective' *Studies in Decentralisation and Quasi-Markets 2*. Bristol: School for Advanced Urban Studies.

Hoggett, P. (1991) 'A new management in the public sector?' *Policy and Politics*, 19(4), 243–56.

Hoggett, P. and Hambleton, R. (eds) (1987) 'Decentralisation and Democracy', *Occasional Paper 28*. Bristol: School for Advanced Urban Studies.

Holliday, I. (1991a) 'The conditions of local change: Kent County Council since reorganisation' *Public Administration*, 69(4), 441–57.

Holliday, I. (1991b) 'The new suburban right in British local government – Conservative views of the local' *Local Government Studies*, 17(6), 45–62.

Houlihan, B. (1988) *Housing Policy and Central–Local Relations*. Aldershot: Avebury.

Hudson, B. (1990) 'Social policy and the new right – the strange case of the community care White Paper' *Local Government Studies*, 16(6), 15–34.

Hudson, R. (1990) 'Trying to revive an infant Hercules: the rise and fall of local authority modernization policies on Teesside', in Harloe, M. *et al.* (eds) *Place, Policy and Politics*. London: Unwin Hyman.

Ibbs Report (1988) *Improving Management in Government: the Next Steps*. Efficiency Unit. London: HMSO.

Jacobs, B. D. (1990a) 'Business leadership in urban regeneration: towards a shared vision?' in King, D. and Pierre, J. (eds) *Challenges to Local Government*. London: Sage.

Jacobs, B. D. (1990b) 'Business leadership in urban regeneration: towards a shared vision?' Paper presented to Political Studies Association, Durham.

Jacobs, B. D. (1992) *Fractured Cities: Capitalism, Community and Empowerment in Britain and American*. London: Routledge.

Jessop, B. (1988) 'Regulation theory, post-Fordism and the state: more than a reply to Werner Bonefeld' *Capital and Class* 34, 147–68.

Jessop, B. (1990) 'Regulation theories in retrospect and prospect' *Economy and Society*, 19(2), 153–216.

Jessop, B. (1991) 'The welfare state in the transition from Fordism to post-Fordism', in Jessop, B. *et al.* (eds) *The Politics of Flexibility: Restructuring State and Industry in Britain, Germany and Scandinavia.* Aldershot: Edward Elgar.

Jessop, B. (1992) 'From the Keynesian welfare state to the Schumpeterian workfare state', Paper presented to *Towards a Post-Fordist Welfare State?* Conference, University of Teesside, 17–18 September.

Jessop, B., Bonnett, K. and Bromley, S. (1989) 'Farewell to Thatcherism? Neo-liberalism and "New Times"' *New Left Review*, 179, 81–103.

Johnson, N. (1987) 'The break-up of consensus: competitive politics in a declining economy', in Loney, M. *et al.* (eds) *The State or the Market.* London: Sage.

Joint Trades Councils (1980) *State Intervention in Industry: A Workers' Inquiry.* Newcastle: Coventy, Liverpool, Newcastle and North Tyneside Trades Councils.

Jones, G. and Stewart, J. (1983) *The Case for Local Government.* London: Allen and Unwin.

Keating, M. (1991) *Comparative Urban Politics: Power and the City in the United States, Canada, Britain and France.* Aldershot: Edward Elgar.

Keith-Lucas, B. and Richards, P. (1978) *A History of Local Government in the Twentieth Century.* London: Allen and Unwin.

Kennedy, R. (1991) *London: World City Moving into the 21st Century. A Research Project.* London: HMSO.

King, D. (1988) 'The next Green Paper on local government finance' *Economic Affairs*, 9(1), 6–12.

King, D. and Pierre, J. (eds) (1990) *Challenges to Local Government.* London: Sage.

King, D. S. (1989) 'The new right, the new left and local government', in Stewart, J. and Stoker, G. (eds) *The Future of Local Government.* London: Macmillan.

Labour Co-ordinating Committee (1981) *Can Local Government Survive?* London: LCC.

Labour Co-ordinating Committee (1984) *Go Local to Survive.* London: LCC.

Labour Co-ordinating Committee (1988) *Labour Councils in the Cold: A Blueprint for Survival.* London: LCC.

LACSAB (1990) *CCT Information Service Survey Report No. 1.* Luton: Local Authorities' Conditions of Service Advisory Board/Local Government Training Board.

Laffin, M. (1986) *Professionalism and Policy: the Role of the Professions in the Central–Local Government Relationship.* Aldershot: Gower.

Lansley, S., Goss, S. and Wintour, P. (1989) *Conflicts in Council: The Rise and Fall of the Municipal Left.* London: Macmillan.

Lash, S. and Urry, J. (1987) *The End of Organized Capitalism.* Cambridge: Polity Press.

Lawless, P. (1989) *Britain's Inner Cities*, 2nd edn. London: Paul Chapman.

Lawless, P. and Raban, C. (eds) (1986) *The Contemporary British City*. London: Harper and Row.

Leach, S., Game, C., Gyford, J. and Midwinter, A. (1986) *The Political Organisation of Local Authorities*. Research Volume 1 of the Widdicombe Committee.

Lee, J. (1963) *Social Leaders and Public Persons: A Study of County Government in Cheshire since 1888*. Oxford: Clarendon Press.

Le Grand, J. (1990) 'Quasi-markets and Social Policy' *Studies in Decentralisation and Quasi-markets 1*. Bristol: School for Advanced Urban Studies.

Lewis, N. (1992) *Inner City Regeneration: The Demise of Regional and Local Government*. Buckingham: Open University Press.

Leys, C. (1989) *Politics in Britain: From Labourism to Thatcherism*, revised edn. London: Verso.

LGTB (1987) *Getting Closer to the Public*. Luton: Local Government Training Board.

Lipietz, A. (1987) *Mirages and Miracles: The Crises of Global Fordism*. London: Verso.

Lipsky, M. (1979) The assault on human services: street-level bureaucrats, accountability and the fiscal crisis, in Greer, S. *et al.* (eds).

Logan, J. and Molotch, H. (1987) *Urban Fortunes: The Political Economy of Place*. Berkeley: University of California Press.

Loney, M. Bocock, R., Clarke, J., Cochrane, A., Graham, P. and Wilson, M. (eds) (1987) *The State or the Market: Politics and Welfare in Contemporary Britain*. London: Sage.

Lorrain, D. (1991) 'Public goods and private operators in France', in Batley, R. and Stoker, G. (eds), *Local Government in Europe: Trends and Developments*. London: Macmillan.

Lowe, P. (1988) 'The reform of the community's structural fund' *Common Market Law Review* 25: 503–21.

Lowndes, V. (1990) '"Thriving on Chaos"? Experiences of decentralisation in an East London borough', paper presented to Political Studies Association Conference, Durham.

Lowndes, V. and Stoker, G. (1992a) 'An evaluation of neighbourhood decentralisation, Part 1: customer and citizen perspectives' *Policy and Politics*, 20, 1: 47–61.

Lowndes, V. and Stoker, G. (1992b) 'An evaluation of neighbourhood decentralisation, Part 2: staff and councillor perspectives' *Policy and Politics*, 20, 2: 143–52.

Macintyre, S. (1980) *Little Moscows: Communism and Working-Class Militancy in Inter-war Britain*. London: Croom Helm.

Mackintosh, M. and Wainwright, H. (1987) *A Taste of Power: The Politics of Local Economics*. London: Verso.

Macrory Report (1970) *Report of the Review Body on Local Government in Northern Ireland*. Belfast: HMSO.

Mallaby Report (1967) *Report of the Committee on the Staffing of Local Government*. London: HMSO.

Mark-Lawson, J., Savage, M., and Warde, A. (1985) 'Gender and local politics: struggles over welfare policies, 1919–1939', in Murgatroyd, L. *et al.*, *Localities, Class and Gender*. London: Pion.

Mark-Lawson, J. and Warde, A. (1987) 'Industrial Restructuring and the Transformation of a Local Political Environment: a Case Study of Lancaster' *Working Paper 33*. Lancaster: Lancaster Regionalism Group.

Martin, R. (1988) 'Industrial capitalism in transition: the contemporary reorganization of the British space-economy' in Massey, D. and Allen, J. (eds), *Uneven Re-development: Cities and Regions in Transition*. London: Hodder and Stoughton.

Massey, D. (1984) *Spatial Divisions of Labour*. London: Macmillan.

Massey, D. and Allen, J. (eds) (1988) *Uneven Re-development: Cities and Regions in Transition*. London: Hodder and Stoughton.

Mather, G. (1989) 'Thatcherism and local government: an evaluation', in Stewart, J. and Stoker, G. (eds) *The Future of Local Government*. London: Macmillan.

Maud Report (1967) *Report of the Committee on the Management of Local Government*. London: HMSO.

McLean, I. (1987) *Public Choice: An Introduction*. Oxford: Blackwell.

Meegan, R. (1988) 'A crisis of mass production?' in Allen, J. and Massey, D. (eds) *The Economy in Question*. London: Sage.

Meegan, R. (1990) 'Merseyside in crisis and conflict', in Harloe, M. *et al.* (eds) *Place, Policy and Politics*. London: Unwin Hyman.

Metcalfe, L. and Richards, S. (1990) *Improving Public Management*, 2nd edn. London: European Institute of Public Administration/Sage.

Midwinter, A. (1988) 'Local budgetary strategies in a decade of retrenchment' *Public Money and Management*, 8(3), 21–8.

Midwinter, A. (1989) 'Economic theory, the poll tax and local spending' *Politics*, 9(2), 9–15.

Midwinter, A., Keating, M. and Taylor, P. (1983) ' "Excessive and unreasonable": the politics of the Scottish hit-list' *Political Studies*, 21(3), 394–417.

Minford, P. (1988) 'How to de-politicise local government' *Economic Affairs*, 9(1), 12–16.

Mishra, R. (1984) *The Welfare State in Crisis: Social Thought and Social Change*. Brighton: Wheatsheaf.

Molotch, H. (1976) 'The city as growth machine' *American Journal of Sociology*, 82(2), 309–30.

Moody, K. (1987) 'Reagan, the business agenda and the collapse of labour', in Miliband, R. *et al.* (eds) *The Socialist Register 1987*. London: Merlin.

Moore, C., Richardson, J., with Moon, J. (1989) *Local Partnership and the Unemployment Crisis in Britain*. London: Unwin Hyman.

Moss Kanter, R. (1989) *When Giants Learn to Dance: Mastering the Challenges of Strategy, Management, and Careers in the 1990s*. London: Unwin Hyman.

Murgatroyd, L. Savage, M., Shapiro, D. *et al.* (1985) *Localities, Class and Gender*. London: Pion.

Murray, R. (1987) *Breaking with Bureaucracy*. Manchester: Centre for Local Economic Strategies.

Murray, R. (1989) 'Fordism and post-Fordism', in Hall, S. and Jacques, M. (eds) *New Times*. London: Lawrence and Wishart.

Murray, C. (1990) *The Emerging British Underclass*. London: IEA Health and Welfare Unit.

Newton, K. and Karran, T. (1985) *The Politics of Local Expenditure*. London: Macmillan.

Niskanen, W. A. (1971) *Bureaucracy and Representative Government*. Chicago: Aldine-Atherton.

Niskanen, W. A. (1973) *Bureaucracy: Servant or Master? Lessons from America*. London: Institute of Economic Affairs.

Offe, C. (1981) 'The attribution of public status to interest groups: observations on the West German case', in Berger, S. *et al.* (eds) *Organizing Interests in Western Europe*. Cambridge: Cambridge University Press.

Offe, C. (1984) *The Contradictions of the Welfare State*. London: Hutchinson.

Painter, J. (1991a) 'Compulsory competitive tendering in local government: the first round' *Public Administration*, 69(2), 191–210.

Painter, J. (1991b) 'Regulation theory and local government' *Local Government Studies*, 17(6), 23–43.

Paterson Report (1973) *The New Scottish Local Authorities: Organization and Management Structures*. Working Group on Scottish Local Authority Management Structures. Edinburgh: HMSO.

Peck, J. (1991) 'Letting the market decide (with public money): Training and Enterprise Councils and the future of labour market programmes' *Critical Social Policy*, 31, 4–17.

Peet, R. and Thrift, N. (eds) (1989) *New Models in Geography, Volume 2: The Political–Economy Perspective*. London: Unwin Hyman.

Perez, C. (1986) 'Structural change and assimilation of new technologies in the economic and social system', in Freeman, C. (ed.) *Design, Innovation and Long Cycles in Economic Development*. London: Pinter.

Peters, T. (1988) *Thriving on Chaos. Handbook for a Management Revolution*. London: Macmillan (page references to Pan paperpack edn, 1989.)

Pickvance, C. (1990) 'Council economic intervention and political conflict in a declining resort: Isle of Thanet', in Harloe, M. *et al.* (eds) *Place, Policy and Politics*. London: Unwin Hyman.

Pickvance, C. (1991) 'The difficulty of control and the ease of structural reform: British local government in the 1980s', in Pickvance, C. and Preteceille, E. (eds) *State Restructuring and Local Power*. London: Pinter.

Pickvance, C. and Preteceille, E. (eds) (1991) *State Restructuring and Local Power: A Comparative Perspective*. London: Pinter.

Pirie, M. (1981) 'Economy and local government', in Butler, E. and Pirie, M. (eds) *Economy and Local Government*. London: Adam Smith Institute.

Pirie, M. (1988) *Micropolitics*. London: Wildwood House.

Pollitt, C. (1986) 'Democracy and bureaucracy', in Held, D. and Pollitt, C. (eds) *New Forms of Democracy*. London: Sage.

Pollitt, C. (1990) *Managerialism and the Public Services: The Anglo-American Experience*. Oxford: Blackwell.

Preston, J. and Hogg, C. (1990) ' "A beast coming out of the mist" – a local government perspective on European Community Integrated Development Operations policy' *Local Government Studies*, 12(6).2, 27–36.

Radley, S. (1992) *A Glimpse of the Future: Social and Economic Trends for Local Government in the 1990s*, The Henley Centre for Forecasting, Luton: Local Government Management Board.

Ranson, S. and Stewart, J. (1989) 'Citizenship and government: the challenge for management in the public domain' *Political Studies*, 37, 5–24.

Ranson, S. and Thomas, H. (1989) 'Education reform: consumer democracy or social democracy?' in Stewart, J. and Stoker, G. (eds) *The Future of Local Government*. London: Macmillan.

Reade, E. (1987) *British Town and Country Planning*. Milton Keynes: Open University Press.

Redcliffe-Maude Report (1969) *Report of the Royal Commission on Local Government*. London: HMSO.

Rhodes, R. (1981) *Control and Power in Central–Local Government Relations*. Farnborough: SSRC/Gower.

Rhodes, R. (1985) ' "A squalid and politically corrupt process?" Intergovernmental relations in the post-war period' *Local Government Studies*, 11(6), 35–57.

Rhodes, R. (1986) ' "Corporate bias" in central–local relations: a case study of the Consultative Council on Local Government Finance' *Policy and Politics*, 14(2), 221–45.

Rhodes, R. (1988) *Beyond Westminster and Whitehall: Sub-Central Governments of Britain*. London: Unwin Hyman.

Rhodes, R. (1991) 'Now nobody understands the system: the changing face of local government', in Norton, P. (ed.) *New Directions in British Politics*. Aldershot: Edward Elgar.

Rhodes, R. (1992) 'Local government finance', in Marsh, D. and Rhodes, R. (eds) *Implementing Thatcherite Policies: Audit of an Era*. Buckingham: Open University Press.

Ridge, M. and Smith, S. (1991) *Local Taxation: the Options and the Arguments*. London: Institute for Fiscal Studies.

Ridley, N. (1988a) *The Local Right: Enabling not Providing*. London: Centre for Policy Studies.

Ridley, N. (1988b) Speech to Conservative Local Government Conference, London, 5 March.

Robins, K. (1990) 'Global local times', in Anderson, J. and Ricci, M. (eds) *Society and Social Science: A Reader*. Milton Keynes: The Open University.

Robson, B. (1988) *Those Inner Cities: Reconciling the Social and Economic Aims of Urban Policy*. Oxford: Clarendon Press.

Robson, W. (1948) *The Development of Local Government*, 2nd edn. London: Allen and Unwin.

Rose, R. (1982) *Understanding the United Kingdom*. London: Longman.

Rustin, M. (1989) 'The politics of post-Fordism: or, the trouble with "New Times"' *New Left Review*, 175, 54–77.

Salmon, P. (1987) 'Decentralisation as an incentive scheme' *Oxford Review of Economic Policy*, 3, 2.

Saunders, P. (1980) *Urban Politics: A Sociological Interpretation*. Harmondsworth: Penguin.

Saunders, P. (1984) 'Rethinking local politics', in Boddy, M. and Fudge, C. (eds) *Local Socialism? Labour Councils and New Left Alternatives*. London: Macmillan.

SAUS (1983) *The Future of Local Democracy*. Bristol: School for Advanced Urban Studies.

Sayer, A. (1989) 'Postfordism in question' *International Journal of Urban and Regional Research*, 13(4) 171–85.

Schmitter, P. (1989) 'Corporatism is dead! Long live corporatism!' *Government and Opposition*, 24(1), 54–73.

Schwarz, B. (1987) 'Conservatives and corporatism' *New Left Review*, 166, 107–28.

SERC (1987) *Lower Don Valley: Final Report*. Sheffield: prepared by Coopers and Lybrand, for the Sheffield Economic Regeneration Committee.

SERC (undated) *Sheffield 2000*. Sheffield Economic Regeneration Committee.

Simmie, J. and French, S. (1989) 'Corporatism, participation and planning: the case of London' *Progress in Planning*, 31(1), 1–57.

Skellington, R. (1993) 'Homelessness', in Dallos, R. and McLaughlin, E. (eds) *Social Problems and the Family*. London: Sage.

Smith, D. (1982) *Conflict and Compromise: Class Formation in English Society 1830–1914. A Comparative Study of Birmingham and Sheffield*. London: Routledge and Kegan Paul.

Smith, D. (1989) 'Customer care and housing services – a practitioner's view', paper presented to Seventh Urban Change and Conflict Conference, Bristol.

Smith, M. P. (1988) *City, State and Market: The Political Economy of Urban Society*. Oxford: Blackwell.

Stewart, J. (1983) *Local Government: The Conditions of Local Choice*. London: Allen and Unwin.

Stewart, J. (1984) 'Storming the town halls: rate capping revolution' *Marxism Today*, 28, 4.

Stewart, J. (1989a) 'The changing organisation and management of local authorities', in Stewart J. and Stoker, G. (eds) *The Future of Local Government*. London: Macmillan.

Stewart, J. (1989b) 'A future for local authorities as community government', in Stewart, J. and Stoker, G. (eds) *The Future of Local Government*. London: Macmillan.

Stewart, J. (1992) 'Guidelines for public service management: lessons not to be learned from the private sector', in Carter *et al.* (eds) *Changing Social Work and Welfare.* Buckingham: Open University Press.

Stewart, J. and Stoker, G. (1988) 'From Local Administration to Community Government' *Fabian Research Series 351,* London: Fabian Society.

Stewart, J. and Stoker, G. (1989a) 'The free local government experiment and the programme of public service reform in Scandinavia', in Crouch, C. and Marquand, D. (eds) *The New Centralism.* Oxford: *The Political Quarterly*/Blackwell.

Stewart, J. and Stoker, G. (eds) (1989b) *The Future of Local Government.* London: Macmillan.

Stewart, J. and Walsh, K. (1989) *The Search for Quality.* Luton: Local Government Management Board.

Stewart, M. (1984) 'Talking to Local Business: the Involvement of Chambers of Commerce in Local Affairs' *Working Paper No. 38,* Bristol: School for Advanced Urban Studies.

Stoker, G. (1988) *The Politics of Local Government.* London: Macmillan.

Stoker, G. (1989a) 'Creating a local government for a post-Fordist society: the Thatcherite project?' in Stewart, J. and Stoker, G. (eds) *The Future of Local Government.* London: Macmillan.

Stoker, G. (1989b) 'Inner cities, economic development and social services: the Government's continuing agenda', in Stewart, J. and Stoker, G. (eds) *The Future of Local Government.* London: Macmillan.

Stoker, G. (1990) 'Regulation theory, local government and the transition from Fordism', in King, D. and Pierre, J. (eds) *Challenge to Local Government.* London: Sage.

Stoker, G. (1991a) *The Politics of Local Government,* 2nd edn. London: Macmillan.

Stoker, G. (1991b) 'Introduction: Trends in Western European local government', in Batley, R. and Stoker, G. (eds) *Local Government in Europe.* London: Macmillan.

Stoker, G. and Wilson, D. (1986) 'Intra-organizational politics in local authorities: towards a new approach' *Public Administration,* 64, 285–302.

Stoker, G. and Wilson, D. (1991) 'The lost world of British local pressure groups', *Public Policy and Administration,* 6(2), 20–34.

Stone, C. (1987) 'The study of the politics of urban development', in Stone, C. and Sanders, H. T. (eds) *The Politics of Urban Development.* Lawrence: University of Kansas Press.

Stone, C. (1989) *Regime Politics. Governing Atlanta, 1946–1988.* Lawrence, Kansas: University of Kansas Press.

Taaffe, P. and Mulhearn, T. (1988) *Liverpool: A City that Dared to Fight.* Liverpool: Fortress Books.

Totterdill, P. (1989) 'Local economic strategies as industrial policy: a critical review of British developments in the 1980s' *Economy and Society,* 18(4), 478–526.

Travers, T. (1989) 'The threat to the autonomy of elected local government,' in Crouch, C. and Marquand, D. (eds) *The New Centalism*. Oxford: *The Political Quarterly*/Blackwell.

Wainwright, H. (1987) *Labour: A Tale of Two Parties*. London: The Hogarth Press.

Warde, A. (1989) 'Recipes for a pudding: A comment on locality' *Antipode*, 21(3), 274–81.

Wheatley Report (1969) Report of the Royal Commission on Local Government in Scotland. Edinburgh: HMSO.

Widdicombe Report (1986) *The Conduct of Local Authority Business: Committee of Inquiry into the Conduct of Local Authority Business*, Cmnd 9797–9801. London: HMSO.

Williams, K., Cutler, T., Williams, J. and Haslam, C. (1987) 'The end of mass production' *Economy and Society*, 16(3), 405–39.

Young, K. (1986) 'Attitudes to local government', in Widdicombe Report, Research Volume III, *The Local Government Elector*.

Young, K. and Davies, M. (1990) *The Politics of Local Government since Widdicombe*. York: Joseph Rowntree Foundation.

Young, K. and Hadley, R. (1990) *Creating a Responsive Public Service*. Hemel Hempstead: Harvester, Wheatsheaf.

Index